the susan southerland secret

everyday brides...extraordinary experiences

The Susan Southerland Secret

Personality Marketing to Today's Bride

Susan Southerland,
Kristy Chenell,
and Karen Gingerich

iUniverse, Inc.
Bloomington

The Susan Southerland Secret
Personality Marketing to Today's Bride

iUniverse books may be ordered through booksellers or by contacting:

iUniverse
1663 Liberty Drive
Bloomington, IN 47403
www.iuniverse.com
1-800-Authors (1-800-288-4677)

Author bio photos and other photos featured within the book were provided courtesy of the following:

Francis Moran Photography
Ginger Midgett Photography
Kim Nodurft Photography
Nu Visions in Photography

ISBN: 978-1-4620-0106-4 (sc)
ISBN: 978-1-4620-0108-8 (hc)
ISBN: 978-1-4620-0107-1 (e)

Printed in the United States of America

iUniverse rev. date: 07/12/2011

Contents

Introduction

*H*ave you ever had a bride call and the first thing she asks is, "How much are your services?" Has her asking this question ever led you to automatically think she wasn't the best fit for your company? Or have you ever used the term "Bridezilla" to describe a client, wishing you had never booked the business in the first place?

What if I told you that these common paradigms could be losing you money and causing you unnecessary stress? I'm here to tell you they are.

Over the years, I have been fortunate to work with thousands of couples as their wedding planner, and now, thanks to my speaking engagements, I get to speak with thousands more every month. This access to couples has offered me distinct insights into their worlds. It has also given me a unique perspective on selling, marketing, and serving couples and their families. Because of this change in my paradigms, my planning company, Just Marry!, increased its sales and lessened stress levels, leading to more than two hundred weddings planned in 2010.

As vendors, we can have a tendency to become stagnant in our perspectives— particularly with brides. We work with them day in and day out, and often identify behavioral trends that don't always appeal to us or our work ethics. I want to help refresh your perspective and help you avoid getting burned out in an industry that is growing rapidly every day and ultimately help you make more money by simply changing the way you understand, identify, and work with different bridal personalities.

The Susan Southerland Secret is a carefully developed method of determining your potential clients' planning and purchasing personality types. By learning how to effectively apply The Susan Southerland Secret to your current marketing and sales efforts, you will be able to hone your business approach. And in so doing, you will increase your company's revenue and reduce overall stress levels for both you and your clients.

Whether you are new to the industry or you have worked in the wedding market for years, the ideas put forth in this book will give you a new outlook on your career path and a renewed confidence and energy in your selling and marketing. This book is not only filled with tips on how to identify a bride's planning personality, but it will also give you ideas that you can implement today to help you increase sales and gain some sanity in your daily work routine.

Susan Southerland

So … how did I get here?

In 1992 I started my wedding planning business in my bedroom at my parents' house with a phone and a desktop computer. I had a full-time job with our local convention and visitors' bureau working with its corporate members. It was through networking with these members that I became known as the "go-to" girl when looking for locations and identifying vendors for weddings. After helping a few acquaintances with their weddings, I realized that I truly enjoyed working with brides and their families in putting their weddings together. So after a few months of working two jobs, I left the security of my full-time gig and started Just Marry!. I haven't looked back since!

Now twenty years later, I have been featured on national television networks such as the Travel Channel, The Learning Channel, and the Style Network. I've been quoted in *The Wall Street Journal*, *The New York Times*, *Orlando Sentinel*, *Orlando Leisure*, *Central Florida Bride*, and *Orlando Business Journal*. In addition, I was featured as one of the thirty A-list destination wedding planners in the world by *Destination Weddings & Honeymoons* magazine. Most recently, I was named the "wedding expert" for the national wedding publication, *Perfect Wedding Guide*.

However, what I am most honored by are the thousands of wedding couples I have worked and spoken with who have put their trust and faith in me. Because of them, I have had the profound opportunity to identify and develop The Susan Southerland Secret: a way to allow everyday brides to have extraordinary experiences through vendors that recognize and produce customized services based on a bride's personality.

When speaking with these thousands of couples, I noticed that they all had great confidence in certain areas of the planning process, while they were very insecure about other areas. For example, some of them thrived on the creative aspects such as their menu and décor, while others were lost in that area, but excelled at keeping a thorough budget and were impeccably organized.

Although each bride I worked with was different, overall trends began to emerge that allowed me to customize my marketing, sales, and overall customer service experience with them. Once I actually put these strengths and weaknesses on paper and designed a strategy around it, I suddenly saw the organization of everything I had previously experienced. I started using the strategies immediately and saw my business grow to over two hundred weddings that very year!

A few years ago, I began working with branding specialist Kristy Chenell. Knowing that I had all of this insight was one thing, but I sought a way to define and share what I had experienced over the years in an easy and understandable way. Through some incredibly fun and insightful branding exercises, Kristy and I discovered a distinct concept, a concept that was easy to explain and that made complete sense each time I met with a bride. It was then a natural progression for us to collaborate with writer and wedding planner, Karen Gingerich, to get the concept into the form of an engaging and helpful book for vendors. We call this concept The Susan Southerland Secret, and I'm excited to share it with you.

"I have to say you are an inspiration to me. You exude happiness and professionalism—qualities everyone desires. I truly aspire to learn from a great wedding planner. Someone like you!"—Anna Ottman, Event Manager

Today's Bride

As you read this book, I encourage you to think openly and take notes on what can be done in your business to begin implementing this new paradigm. Whether big or small, each change and new way of looking at today's bride can make a significant impact on your bottom line. And ultimately, that's what we are all in business to do.

Chapter 1: Who Is Today's Bride?

"Today" is a relevant term. In an industry that constantly introduces new brides over the years, that also means new generations. As we get older, the age difference between our clientele and us thus becomes greater and greater. Many times, we think we know and understand the new generation with whom we are working, but as we lead our busy lives and try to keep up with the latest trends in our respective specialties (photography, floral, planning, etc.), how do we continue to keep up with who "today's" bride really is in regard to her ideals, her preferences, her buying styles, etc.?

After extensive research on the elements and traits of today's bride, I understand how the challenges we face as vendors are heavily influenced by the changing dynamics of a new generation. In learning more about this upcoming generation, we are preparing ourselves more strategically in marketing and sales, with an ultimate goal of making more money and lessening our stress.

Identifying with Echo Boomers

Let's face it—we have a variety of challenges that we face each day just from being part of a small business. However, the majority of vendors that I speak with say that marketing and sales are two of the areas of greatest concern for their companies. That's not a surprise given the new generation of Echo Boomers we are now working with and the preferences and priorities that they have and expect.

Vendors today have the notable challenge of marketing and selling to a generation of brides who were born into a diverse, high-tech world. Known collectively as Echo Boomers, Generation Y, or the Millennials, today's brides and grooms are not only used to technological change and economic competition, they expect it. Because of this, the landscape is changing for the way we market and conduct our businesses.

Even more, with the Echo Boomer generation containing more minorities and a wider economic spread than any previous generation, today's vendors need to adjust their marketing and sales strategies to compensate if they want their businesses to succeed.

Born between 1979 and 2002, Echo Boomers are the children of the Baby Boomers. With an estimated 71 million of them on the scene, Echo Boomers represent the largest generation since their parents'. Though they're the offspring of the Baby Boomers, don't mistake their tastes and attitudes for Mom and Dad's. Unlike tradition-bucking Baby Boomers, Echo Boomers are often described as "neo-traditionalists." They believe in marriage and they want a traditional wedding, but they want to put their own spin on it. Traditional religious ceremony? Sure, say some Echo Boomers. Complete with the standard house of worship cantor? No, thanks. Flying in a musician the couple heard on a recent vacation is more appealing to these sophisticated pairs.

Echo Boomers are also more tech-savvy than any group before them. This is, after all, a generation who doesn't know life without fast computers, tiny cell phones, or the Internet (and we don't mean dial-up!). Echo Boomers embrace technologies like e-mail, texting, and instant messaging (IMing). These brides and grooms are much more likely to e-mail a potential wedding vendor for information than to pick up the phone and call. Additionally, creating websites, joining online communities, storing their music on iPods, and burning their own CDs and DVDs are second nature to the Echo Boomers and impact the way they plan their weddings.

Dum, Dum, Da Dum: The Impact of Echo Boomers on the Wedding Industry

The oldest Echo Boomers—those around twenty-eight and twenty-nine years old—are just starting to tie the knot in large numbers, and their presence and particular way of navigating life are revolutionizing the wedding industry.

First, there is the fact that there are so many of them: "In the next fifteen years, the number of Echo Boomers turning twenty-seven (the average age for women to marry) will grow 22 percent. Assuming that the average age of a bride and other factors remain constant, an increase in marriages seems likely due to the sheer size of the group," reports the Fairchild Bridal Group, publishers of *Bride's*, *Modern Bride*, and *Elegant Bride* magazines ("The American Wedding," 2004). Second, they have significant resources. A 2007 study by VISA USA estimates that by the year 2015, the Echo Boomer generation will account for approximately $2.45 trillion in annual spending, some of which will be devoted to planning their weddings.

In general, Echo Boomers differ from engaged couples before them in several ways. Here are the biggies:

- **They're older.** Over the last forty years, the average age of marrying couples has risen steadily. Today, the median age of a bride is twenty-seven and a groom twenty-nine, according to the Fairchild Bridal Group.
- **They've been exposed.** An explosion of television shows such as *Whose Wedding Is It Anyway?*, *Platinum Weddings*, *Rich Bride, Poor Bride*, *Weddings Away*, and *Bridezillas*—as well as televised "celebrity" weddings—has given Echo Boomers an unprecedented look behind the scenes at what goes into planning a wedding, and the possible results. Because of this, Echo Boomers care a lot about making their weddings "perfect" and "unforgettable."
- **They're more pragmatic in their spending.** We wouldn't dare call them cheap—they aren't, by any means—but Echo Boomers

do place a premium on getting a good value for their money. In the VISA study, 83 percent of Echo Boomers identified themselves as bargain shoppers and 80 percent said they stick to a strict budget when making purchases.

- **They're more diverse.** Men and women of this generation are more likely to marry outside of their own religious or ethnic groups than ever before.
- **Their definition of "couple" is broader.** They recognize partnerships between two men and two women instead of strictly a man and a woman.
- **They take a more global view of wedding planning.** Whether it means tying the knot at a distant spot (i.e., a destination wedding) or searching far beyond the borders of their wedding locale for talented wedding pros, Echo Boomers see no reason to be restricted by geography.
- **They're more influenced by word-of-mouth than traditional advertising.** These couples have grown up with plenty of screen-time—from TV to the Internet—and are extremely media savvy. They hate "being sold," but are significantly moved by recommendations from their peers. According to a Nielsen Global Online Consumer Survey of over 25,000 Internet consumers from fifty countries, 90 percent of consumers surveyed noted that they trust recommendations from people they know, while 70 percent trusted consumer opinions posted online ("Global Advertising," 2009).

We've Got a Front-Row Seat

As a wedding planner, I'm seeing firsthand how our Echo Boomer clients are approaching wedding planning from a fresh perspective. For instance, there was a time when I primarily worked with the bride and her mother (who wielded a lot of decision-making power since she controlled the checkbook). Over time, the groom became a more active player and helped choose menus, musicians, and more. These days, grooms still play an important role, but my Echo Boomer brides are as likely to bring their best friends along to meetings with me as they are to show up with their moms or fiancés. This is part of a bigger trend: Echo Boomers have very close relationships with their peers and are often involved in helping to plan each other's weddings. Today's bride may be in several other weddings across the country at the same time she's planning her own. This presents some unique opportunities and challenges.

Another huge trend related to Echo Boomers is the increase in couples marrying outside of their faith and/or ethnicity. For that reason, they have a keen interest in finding special ways to combine the traditions of the bride and groom's cultures and religions into their wedding. I recently planned a wedding that beautifully integrated the bride's Vietnamese heritage with the groom's Irish background. (Think a chic bamboo altar, bagpipers, flower girls scattering four-leaf clovers, and a feast featuring Lychee martinis, shot glasses of potato leek soup, and petite corned beef sandwiches). I've planned numerous weddings that blended Jewish and Christian elements (often presided over by a rabbi and a minister or priest), as well as Hindu-Christian weddings pairing a traditional Christian wedding ceremony with traditional Indian dress and preceremony henna painting on the bride's hands.

I am also seeing a big change in what couples feel constitutes a wedding. The options have expanded far beyond the usual church, garden, or hotel ceremony followed by dinner and dancing. Today, a couple might opt for a bountiful brunch, a swank cocktail party, or a decadent all-dessert reception. Perhaps they'll jet off for a destination wedding with family and friends in tow. Or maybe they'll elope and then host a big bash when they return home. Some couples are even opting for a private ceremony for just their closest friends and relatives followed by a blow-out reception for hundreds.

In addition, Echo Boomers have an eye on Hollywood. This generation has grown up poring over celebrity magazines such as *People, InStyle,* and

US Weekly, and they have their BlackBerries set to Perezhilton.com and TMZ.com to kill time with celebrity news while waiting in line or at a stoplight. As a result, they're greatly influenced by their favorite stars' weddings and other parties and are eager to find ways to recreate celebrity bashes—though usually on a more modest budget!

Echo Boomers have grown up in a culture where they are constantly inundated with information. Have you ever noticed how short many of their attention spans are? There is so much available at their fingertips that they don't have to linger long on a website, a television or radio station, or even a magazine before flipping to the next, most intriguing thing.

This is why marketing messages must be clever and expertly delivered to have any impact. After all, effective advertising is extremely difficult in a society where spam filters reject all but the most innocuous e-mail messages, television commercials go unseen using TiVo or another DVR, and even radio ads are ignored by flipping the station or streaming XM radio. Vendors working with this generation of brides and grooms certainly face some unique challenges.

When was the last time you watched or listened to an entire commercial or read a complete magazine advertisement?

What was it about it that kept your interest?

Planning Echo Boomer Weddings

In regard to planning their weddings, Echo Boomers have a keen interest in achieving trendy looks, and they want their wedding vendors to identify the most affordable (or most bang-for-their-buck) ways to achieve that. With an increasing amount of vendors to select from, Echo Boomers have the fortunate opportunity to search until they can find just the right team to pull off the newest trends at prices that offer them the most value for what they spend.

Design/Trends

Have you ever asked a bride what her vision is for her wedding day and she answers with, "Simple, yet elegant," only to realize that there is much more extravagance and details once the planning begins? It happens to me all the time.

I could write about all of the latest trends that are "simple, yet elegant" that I've seen, as well as what I think may be most popular for the next few years, but with Echo Boomers, it's not that easy. With them, it's all about one thing: customization. Today's couples want to feel that their wedding is unique, that it's a reflection of them, and that it is unlike what any bride has done before (even if you as a vendor have seen it before), and it goes beyond just having something monogrammed.

It's crucial that we keep this in mind as we market and sell to today's bride. Even though we may see certain trends emerge, it's important that we sell or customize the idea to each couple. Some of the best salespeople I've witnessed in consultations are those vendors who can sell the same space, the same bouquet, the same package over and over again in a way that makes it seem as though the current couple is the first to experience anything like it and that it was made for them.

How can you customize your current packages?

How can you personalize each of your consultations?

Budgeting

Gone are the days when the parents of the bride footed the entire bill for the wedding. Now the cost is often shared by both sets of parents and/or grandparents, and just as often directly shouldered by the bride and groom. Because of this and the effects of the economy, the cost of wedding services is more of a factor than it has been in decades.

There is much information available regarding the average cost of weddings, and I do see that fluctuate slightly every year. However, with the Echo Boomer generation, overall cost seems to be less of a predictor on whether they will purchase your services than their list of priorities. Echo Boomer couples vary significantly on their lists of priorities. For example, some couples rank photography as number one on their list of importance and are willing to spend high to get the quality they want. Because of this, they are willing to forgo things such as videography, a band, or even their dream honeymoon in order to get exactly what they want for their first priority.

What is both fun and challenging at the same time is that each couple (not to mention each bride and groom separately) has their own individual priorities and preferences. Just as one couple prefers to spend the majority of their budget on the reception, another one may elect to spend it on paying for ten of their closest friends and family to travel to Europe for a small, intimate ceremony.

I hear many vendors say that they only prefer to contract weddings that have a certain minimum budget ($50,000, for example). While in theory this may result in excellent photographs of the weddings to share with others, there is no predicting how an Echo Boomer will spend that $50,000 budget. It could possibly be spent on an element such as extraordinary wines because that happens to be a passion of the couple, or maybe the majority of their budget will be used for a top-rated band so their guests can dance the night away. This isn't the case every time, but it is noteworthy to mention, as I have witnessed many vendors lose sales because of this perspective.

In Defense of Today's Bride
Throughout the year, I travel consistently, speaking with wedding vendors across the country and listening to their industry comments and concerns. Over the past ten years, I have seen a trend in complaining about nasty brides, clueless brides, overbearing brides, and flaky brides—the ultimate "Bridezillas." After noticing that this was at the forefront of vendors' minds from coast to coast, I confess that I found it concerning, and I started wondering why this conversation was becoming so common.

This is why I find it crucial to look inside the mind of a bride. For a moment, let's take into consideration what brides are faced with when planning weddings today.

Their Friends' Expectations: The Echo Boomer generation holds their peers in the highest regard. Most often, the bride and groom's friends have a greater impact on their decision-making process than their parents. They also tend to have very large circles of friends, which makes for a great deal of opinions to sort through.

When I think of the friends' sphere of influence, I think of a trip that I took to a gown salon with one of my brides—we'll call her Laura. Laura brought an entourage of ten women with her: her mom, her maid of honor, four bridesmaids, four classmates, and me. I sat back to watch the interaction that took place among Laura and her group. First, she would pick a gown that she liked and then would hold it up for the group to see. If there was even one negative reaction, the gown would go back on the rack. When five or six gowns finally met with everyone's approval, Laura went into the dressing room to try them on. She would then emerge from the dressing room and not even glance in the mirror. Her entire focus was on her group's reactions. Again, one nose wrinkle and the gown came off, never to be seen again, regardless of how much she truly liked it.

Their Parents' Expectations: Mom and Dad aren't completely out-of-the loop when it comes to influencing the decisions couples make when planning their weddings. Even if the bride and groom are paying for the wedding themselves, they are still influenced by what their parents think. I find parental influences emerge mostly when the couple wants to try something new or different. For example, destination weddings tend to get a negative parental response, as do weddings outside of either the bride's or groom's place of worship. This has much to do with the previous generation's focus on tradition.

A few years ago, I had a client, April, who had a very involved mother. April's mother attended absolutely every appointment. One day, we met at my office to discuss April's vision for her décor. We discussed colors, linen types, lighting, and of course, flowers. She had a very detailed vision of what she wanted. After two hours of sharing photos and giving detailed explanations of exactly what she wanted (surprisingly with almost no input from her mother), the appointment was over. They were out of my office for about five minutes when my phone rang. It was April's mother. She said, "Susan, that was a great meeting, but we aren't going to do any of what we discussed. I'll e-mail you the details of how I want the room to look." Within an hour, I had four pages of notes and photo attachments.

When we went to the florist, her mother's images and notes were the ones that we used and nothing that April wanted was mentioned again. The wedding was beautiful, but not at all what the bride had envisioned. April later told me that the décor just wasn't important enough to her for her to disappoint her mom.

Media Pressure: I have found the media to be most influential in both positive and negative ways on today's couples. At any given time, couples can find something about weddings on television, online, and in magazines. They don't have to search very long to find something interesting! However, in each of these genres, they are consistently bombarded with images of multimillion dollar weddings and poor behavior.

The pressure to make one's wedding equally as extravagant (on a shoestring budget) as what is seen in the media is huge. Shows and ads make it seem so easy, don't they? Many brides are quite shocked when they learn the actual prices.

The question then is: *what elements of those weddings does a bride want?*

A bride wants to look like those brides (weight-loss pressure), she wants the wedding to look like those weddings (monetary pressure), and ultimately, she wants to feel the same way those brides appear to (utterly blissful).

Today's bride wants to emulate the look and feel of those weddings, no matter how orchestrated or unrealistic they may be. It is the *feeling* they desire. Unfortunately, what many brides don't realize is that many of these television shows, magazine articles, and blog posts are photo shoots. If you've ever tried to recreate a picture, you understand how it may take three hours to get just the right shot with the perfect lighting. Brides don't see pictures and automatically know it was shot in a studio and then edited and touched up to make the perfect picture for an editor. On top of that, many budgets for a photo shoot picture of one centerpiece can be as much as the cost of fifteen of those centerpieces at a real wedding.

One of the most interesting comments I ever heard about the sort of pressure placed on brides by the media was at a national wedding conference I recently attended. One of the presentations was done by a well-known magazine that publishes many DIY ideas. They stated very frankly that most of the projects they place in their magazine are meant to be taken to professional florists to create rather than the bride because they are so difficult. Hmm.

In addition to making the difficult and expensive look easy and affordable, the media has also glamorized poor behavior. It's not hard to find a television show that boasts brides screaming at their bridal party for not losing enough weight, or a groom yelling at a limousine driver for taking a wrong turn.

Watching these shows can often influence the behavior of some of the brides with whom we work. It's important that we keep this in mind and be mindful of what behavior we will accept and what we will not, and to be clear about this when booking a client.

Pressure from Within: Many of the couples that I meet are not only planning weddings, but they are changing jobs, building houses, finishing school … the list goes on and on. They are pressed for time, they lack sleep, and they feel like they have to create the event of the decade.

My point is that sometimes we have to excuse bad behavior. I don't mean that we have to take abuse, but it can sometimes be beneficial to give brides the benefit of the doubt before jumping to our own assumptions. Also, by understanding the four planning personalities, you will be able to more effectively communicate with your clients, and you will be better able to manage your own stress when "Bridezilla" comes through your door.

The good news? Echo Boomers represent a significant increase in the overall US population compared to their predecessors, Generation X. In fact, Echo Boomers rival the Baby Boomer generation in population growth, falling only 3 percent short in matching their numbers (Zaldivar 1998). That means the pool of potential clients for vendors is higher than it has been in an entire generation.

So, what does this have to do with The Susan Southerland Secret? The answer: everything.

The majority of the brides you are targeting with your marketing and sales efforts are Echo Boomers, and each has her own planning personality. By being mindful that today's bride wants flexibility and choice and she wants it *yesterday*, you can learn to attract her easily distracted interest, resulting in increased sales. By identifying her planning personality and targeting your sales and marketing efforts specifically to that, you will secure her interest, respect, and business.

"In all my years working in the wedding and event industry, nothing has given me a fresher and more useful perspective on today's bride than The Susan Southerland Secret."—Bonnie Garfield, director of catering, Loews Portofino Bay Hotel

Chapter 2: What Is The Susan Southerland Secret?

After years of working with brides, I began to notice that sometimes the selling process was straightforward: meet, chat, book. Other times, it was meet, chat, send examples, negotiate contract, renegotiate contract, and book. Planning went the same way. Sometimes it was quick, thorough, and efficient, and other times it was a long, excruciating battle.

There were days that I would sit and review what I accomplished in a week and I would notice that one bride would take three times as much of my time as another for the same task. There were ten times the number of e-mails, twice as many calls, and still no decisions were made. I was relatively sure that my planning style didn't change from one client to the next, so I reasoned that it must have something to do with the planning styles of my clients. Then I set about trying to figure out how I could identify and classify those different planning styles.

When it comes to planning weddings, I realized that tasks in their simplest forms can be broken down into "Art" and "Business." Almost every element of planning a wedding falls into one of these two categories, aiding us in recognizing a bride's strengths and weaknesses.

Art

The "Art" of planning a wedding includes everything that involves the look and feel of the day (e.g., flowers and decor, attire, food, music, photography, videography, and hair and makeup). These are thought of many times as the "pretty things," and are the foundation of many wedding magazines, blogs, and television shows.

Something to note about the "Art" side of weddings is that these aspects of a wedding are very subjective. There is no clear "right or wrong," and a bride's opinion is just as valid as a vendor's opinion even though they may be completely different. This means that just because we think something is beautiful doesn't mean a bride has the same eye or knowledge that we do. If she thinks something is gorgeous, who are we to say it isn't?

> Keep in mind that beauty truly is in the eye of the beholder and that we, as vendors, are simply the catalysts that provide beauty a bride desires.

Business

The "Business" of planning a wedding includes all of the organizational aspects of planning, i.e., budgeting, guest list creating, interviewing, hiring, contract negotiating, and organizing the wedding day. These elements are sometimes considered the "professional" side of planning and can many times cause stress or drama featured on television shows or written about in online forums. Unlike the Art aspects, the Business side of weddings is much more black and white. This deals with "yes and no" and is crucial to your business model.

Bringing It All Together

Over the years, I have discovered that some couples find both the Art and the Business aspects of wedding planning easy, some find only the Business easy, some find only the Art easy. And still others find both aspects equally challenging. Because I noticed these trends, I eventually started administering quizzes specifically designed to determine each couple's strengths and weaknesses. Not only did it help my team sell and plan differently (and with much more ease) with each couple, but it opened each couple's eyes to what they truly needed help with and where they could save money doing specific things on their own. This concept and our created system worked beautifully, and that is how The Susan Southerland Secret concept was developed.

Why Is It Important to You?

Why should you care about a bride's strengths and weaknesses? Well, let's consider today's bride, discussed in the previous chapter. The generation of brides to whom we are now selling is immune to traditional marketing efforts. They have been bombarded with advertisements and sales pitches. Because of this, they don't trust everything they see and hear in magazines, television, and radio. Considering these are the traditional avenues of marketing, what are you to do? The Susan Southerland Secret opens up the ability to connect with the bride based on how she thinks or what she worries about in order to make a personal connection, which in turn makes her more likely to choose to work with you.

Brides today are also looking for personal experiences when it comes to planning and executing their weddings. They want their experiences to be their own, something to tell their friends about, something that is exclusive to just them (even if they do bring you pictures of another wedding that they want to duplicate!). Having insight into a bride's personality through her strengths and weaknesses will allow you to service her wedding in an easy, customized manner. Not only does a personalized experience with you provide you a happy (and many times calmer) bride, but this is crucial in getting referrals—the easiest and cheapest way to market yourself!

As I mentioned in the prior chapter, friends are a crucial part of decision making for the Echo Boomer generation. This means that if a bride hires you and considers you a fantastic "find," she'll tell everyone she knows, and you are more likely to be hired by her friends for future weddings.

A few years ago, I saw three brides in the same circle of friends who selected the same location to have their wedding receptions. Even though there are hundreds of locations within the city, each of them selected the same venue—one of the top wedding sites in town—because they were all so impressed. Each wedding was distinctly different in style, but because they each found it a fabulous "find," they all celebrated their weddings there within one year.

What Is It?

The Susan Southerland Secret is a method of determining what type of planning and purchasing personality your potential client has. Once you have determined your potential client's personality type, you will be able to tailor your sales and service tactics to match that personality.

One caveat: I am not encouraging you to be deceptive; rather, The Susan Southerland Secret is a way to understand and empathize with your client's needs and therefore work with her more effectively. A bride will be able to tell if you are being manipulative or deceitful. If you are unable to work with a particular bride based on what she is looking for, be prepared to refer her to a trusted colleague who more closely fits her needs.

How Can It Help Me?

Sales, marketing, and servicing is no longer one-size-fits-all. You must be able to recognize what your client or potential client needs in order to be able to stand out from others in your industry. Competition in the wedding industry is fierce, and today's bride knows how to find exactly what she is looking for. In order to stay competitive, you need to learn to adapt.

In addition, how much money do you typically set aside each year for your marketing and sales strategies? Unless you have an endless supply of capital, it's crucial to be smart in how you spend your allotted dollars. The Susan Southerland Secret lays out a strategic plan that you can adapt based on your budget, goals, and brand.

When Can I Use It?

Vendors who have worked with The Susan Southerland Secret have used it during bridal shows, sales calls, advertising design, and throughout the entire working process with their clients. It has provided them with new perspectives on how to communicate with brides, from the very first phone call to the negotiation and contract signing process.

Awareness of your clients' strengths and weaknesses will serve you in every aspect of your business. It allows us as vendors to appeal very specifically to potential clients by tailoring sales and marketing messages to each bride. Furthermore, this knowledge helps us cope with the months of planning ahead, which can greatly reduce stress and lead to a more effective working relationship with the client.

Let's put ourselves there for a moment. When you think of how you deal with your own company, consider if the following comments apply to you:

> *I'm great at my craft, but dealing with conflict makes me want to hide under my desk!*
> Or, *I don't mind preparing proposals and contracts, but answering the phone intimidates me!*
> Or maybe even, *I love being a small business owner. I just wish I had the ability to delegate more tasks so I had more time to myself!*

Do any of these sound familiar?

Like all of us, brides and grooms have varying skill levels. Their strengths and weaknesses determine what type of bride or groom they are.

I have developed the following table to depict the Art and Business categories and how strengths and weaknesses in each category identify the different planning personalities.

Table 1: Identifying Planning Personalities by Category

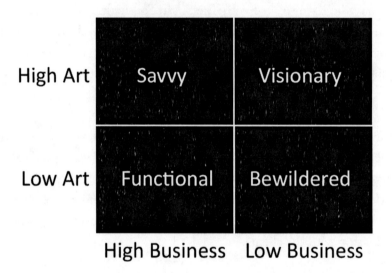

	High Business	Low Business
High Art	Savvy	Visionary
Low Art	Functional	Bewildered

Savvy Brides
We call brides who are confident on both the Business and Art side of planning the wedding Savvy brides. They generally feel comfortable in both areas and enjoy planning every aspect of their weddings.

Functional Brides
Brides who are confident in the Business side of planning a wedding but are insecure about bringing out the Art side are known as Functional

brides. They have a tendency to be more right-brained and focused on hard facts.

Visionary Brides

We call those who are insecure in the Business side of planning a wedding but are very eloquent when discussing the Art side Visionary brides. These brides have expressive personalities and typically visually beautiful weddings.

Bewildered Brides

The Bewildered bride is unsure about both the Business and Art side of planning a wedding. She may either be challenged in both areas or sometimes just doesn't have enough time to focus on either area.

As vendors, we can also use these guidelines to identify our own strengths and weaknesses. For example, I myself am naturally Functional. But as a wedding planner, I have had to strengthen my Visionary side so that I can best relate to all of the brides I work with on every level.

"It's been almost five years since I was a bride, and I think at the time I was a Functional bride all the way! I had spreadsheets for everything, had a line-by-line budget with detailed notes, and knew my vendor contracts inside and out. The downside, though, was that because I was so 'Functional,' I didn't think anyone could coordinate or plan my wedding better than me, so I did it all myself. Now, looking back on my wedding, that is the biggest regret I have—not hiring someone to handle the details and help pull out the 'Visionary' aspects I know are inside me. But the experience has also helped me immediately relate to Functional brides. I know what their concerns are, what their thought processes are, and I know exactly how to 'speak their language.' But, if it wasn't for Susan's secrets, I would have never identified any of that!"—Lindsy Hines, coordinator and owner, Weddings by Lindsy

Curious to know your planning personality? Go to <u>www.susansoutherland</u> <u>.com</u> or see appendix A and take the Planning Personality quiz. Later, we'll go into more detail about how you can learn to identify your strengths and weaknesses and make adjustments to overcome any deficiencies in sales, marketing, and customer service.

First Encounters: A Tale of Four Brides

To give you a better picture of what you can expect when interacting with the four different planning personalities, I'd like to share a few stories with you about some of my past brides. Note: names have been changed to protect the innocent!

Jane (A Savvy Bride)

When I first met Jane and her mother, I was surprised and overwhelmed with all of the information they had for me. They had a timeline for their tasks, an overall budget broken down into what they were going to spend for each vendor, swatches of fabric that they liked, photos of flowers, dresses, and place settings that they wanted … honestly, they had everything in perfect order, neatly organized into two accordion files.

My first thought was, "Why do they need me?" They had done such a wonderful job planning everything that they wanted and they knew exactly how they were going to pay for it. *But* both Mom and Jane wanted to be able to relinquish control to someone capable on the wedding day. They needed vendors they could trust to carry out all of their plans precisely as they wanted them.

Jane was a classic Savvy bride. Like most Savvies, Jane was a self-described overachiever who knew what she wanted and how she was going to accomplish it. What she needed was to surround herself with vendors she trusted so that she could relax and enjoy all of her efforts.

Lisa (A Functional Bride)

Lisa and her fiancé came to me with perfectly planned guest lists, budgets calculated to the last penny, and most of their vendor contracts already negotiated. However, Lisa was stuck on the look of her wedding. She was so frustrated. She told me that she had been digging through magazines and scouring websites for inspiration, but no inspiration came. It was important to her (as it is to most brides) that her wedding was stylish and reflective of their personalities as a couple. She desperately needed help bringing out her "inner artist."

Ultimately, we had to visit twelve florists before Lisa finally connected with one who worked well with her. This particular vendor relationship was so effective because the vendor used pictures and "high-gain" questions in an effort to really understand her. He asked about her home décor, the clothes she liked to wear, and similar questions that truly helped him define her vision. In the end, the flowers turned out absolutely stunning, and Lisa knew to the penny how much she had spent for each petal she got!

Lisa's planning style identified her as a Functional bride. She needed vendors who could help her realize and execute her vision. As with most Functionals, Lisa benefited from vendors who used creative ways to bring out the vision that she herself couldn't identify.

Stacey (A Visionary Bride)
Stacey was perfectly clear on how her wedding was going to look. She could sketch pictures of her gown, her flowers, and her centerpieces. She had a good idea of the food she wanted to serve and the music that she wanted to play. She, however, had no idea what things cost, whether or not she could afford them, and what the process of interviewing and contracting vendors was going to be like. She needed a business manager!

When I work with my clients on their budgets, I find it helpful to give them low-, medium-, and high-budget options to choose from in each vendor category. In Stacey's case, she was consistently selecting options in the high-budget category. I had met with Stacey and her fiancé and assumed they were making these choices together until I received a late-night phone call from the groom explaining that he was quite frustrated with being so over budget. As a result of that call, I spent hours renegotiating vendor contracts to bring them back within their budget. Lesson learned!

As a Visionary bride, Stacey needed extra guidance in budgeting and task management. As a result, she was very open to suggestions on where and how to spend her money. Visionaries with ample budgets are among the very best clients a vendor can have because they are very open to upselling. If she sees something that she decides she has to have, she will almost always go for it. However, a Visionary bride with a limited budget (or sometimes even one with an ample budget!) has a tendency to overspend based on emotion without considering the bottom line and may in the future have to renegotiate her contracts in order to not go into debt.

Tiffany (A Bewildered Bride)
Tiffany contacted me after attempting to plan her wedding for months, as she was so overwhelmed. She tried to put together a guest list, but didn't know how to organize it or who to add and who to leave off. She tried to create a budget, but she didn't know what things cost or how to go about finding that out. She really didn't even know overall how much she had to spend.

As far as how she wanted the wedding to look, every time she picked out a color combination, one of her friends would say something negative that caused her to second-guess her decision. She had no clue what flowers she liked and she hadn't even begun to think about a menu. And on top of everything else, she couldn't even decide on a venue.

Tiffany was most definitely a Bewildered bride. Bewildereds can be the most challenging to work with because they are so unsure of the decisions they make and they are so eager to please everybody. I'll admit that when I first started working with Bewildered brides, I thought of them as manipulative. I couldn't believe that anyone could wrestle so much with each decision. But over time, I have come to realize that there is a genuine sense of insecurity on behalf of the Bewildered bride when it comes to planning her wedding. Bewildereds will be the most time-consuming clients to work with, taking patience and understanding. If you can withstand the trials of working with a Bewildered bride, you will have an extraordinarily grateful client. So be sure to follow up with her to get that glowing letter of reference!

What To Take Away from This

I have had vendors say to me in the past that much of this would fall on a wedding planner's shoulders. I have a very simple answer for that: most brides don't use wedding planners. Every single wedding vendor has an opportunity to help a bride balance her weaknesses so that she can have an amazing wedding.

For now, you need to know that helping a bride feel comfortable with the wedding planning process will make you stand out from your competition. If you take the time to get to know a potential bride, you will be able to win her confidence and get her business. As you work with her throughout the months of planning her wedding, you will be able to find opportunities to upsell her on other services that she needs, and you will feel relaxed in the planning process yourself when she gets uptight.

Chapter 3: The Savvy Bride

*P*icture this: everything is perfect at the church. The flowers are gorgeous, the guests are anxiously awaiting the start of the ceremony, and the entire wedding party looks amazing and is beautifully dressed. Then the music begins to play. It's incredibly emotional.

The minister and the groomsmen all file into their spots at the altar and then the bridesmaids begin their processional down the aisle. You and the bride are watching everything unfold from the back of the church.

Now it's time for the bride to process. Herald trumpeters take their cue to play "Trumpet Voluntary," announcing the bride's processional. Goosebumps appear on your arms from the dramatic emotion that the trumpets evoke.

You arrange the bride's cathedral-length train as she takes her father's arm and prepares to process. He has tears in his eyes. What a stunning moment.

As the bride goes to take her first step down the aisle, she turns to look at you. You expect her to say, "I'm so excited!" or "This is so amazing!"

Instead, she says, "Make sure the reception site folded the napkins correctly."

This story epitomizes the Savvy bride. And it's true … it happened to me.

Savvy Strengths

Good decision maker. If the Savvy bride is the one actually paying for the wedding, she may make decisions right on the spot. Most likely she will have done a great deal of homework before visiting with you and she will know how your services and prices compare to others in the industry. So, if you're able to win her over in a sales presentation, she may very well sign right then.

Craves creativity. A Savvy bride is up to new things. If you keep up on the latest trends and go for continuing education and you know what's hot, she'll be ready to try it out. This is not only good for your portfolio, but it can also be very lucrative. If there's something you've always wanted to do, the Savvy bride is definitely the one you want to approach with the idea.

Fair negotiator. Let's not forget that a Savvy bride knows how to deal with money. She is very likely to want to understand in detail what she is paying for and why. She will most likely want to negotiate for the best deal she can get, but she will not ask you to work for nothing.

Uber-organized. The Savvy bride will keep notes and e-mails and pictures and drawings throughout the planning process. If she has deadlines to keep, she will keep them. She definitely won't need babysitting.

Savvy Weaknesses

Challenges with giving up control. A Savvy has a desire to control every element that goes into her wedding. For vendors, this can reinforce our feelings of inadequacy because she will ask a lot of questions and she will check up on us to make sure things are done correctly.

Ever-planning. As demonstrated in my above story, a Savvy bride may never be finished planning her wedding. Throughout the entire day, she'll be asking herself, "Is this done correctly?" and "What should we be doing now?" I have many times experienced a Savvy bride with hair and makeup half-done, in sweatpants and a button-down shirt, running around the reception room checking to make sure everything looks as planned.

Selling to a Savvy Bride

The Savvy bride is a wonderful blend of the Functional bride and Visionary bride. She knows what she wants and is out to find the perfect vendors to help her achieve her vision in a way that fits her budget.

Her buys are both fact-based and emotion-based. She wants to ensure that the vendor's service or product she's purchasing is a perfect fit emotionally and makes her feel good. But she also needs to have that purchase be a reasonable fit. She knows that if she spends over her budget on the vendor that made her feel most comfortable during the consultation, she'll regret going over that budget a month from now.

She knows her stuff. Similar to the Functional bride, the Savvy bride may know more about what's going on in the world of weddings than you do at the current moment. She has her favorite blogs bookmarked and she reads every wedding magazine front to back the day it comes in the mail. When she meets with you, her favorite pages and ideas are printed out, bookmarked, and organized.

Savvies know what they like and how they want it to look. She may ask for your advice, but be careful not to negate her ideas. She has worked hard to create her vision and will pretty much stick to it. If one of her ideas won't work well from your viewpoint, ask her questions to see if she has thought about every aspect. Then, provide her with some options in case she hasn't. If it becomes her idea to change something, it will allow her to stay in control.

She wants to know that you know your stuff. Savvy brides want to know that you're as knowledgeable about your business and industry as she is. If you've been featured in a magazine, on a blog, on a television or radio show, are asked to speak at conferences, or are even on a preferred vendor list for other vendors or venues, this is the bride to tell it to. She'll appreciate your expertise and many times won't mind stretching her budget if needed for a vendor as talented as you.

There's a local florist used frequently by one of my associates who has utilized her bathroom for strengthening this exact concept. Located in her small bathroom is a beautiful shelving unit across from the toilet. On those shelves sit gorgeous frames with magazine layouts featuring her work. Even though she has other magazine features throughout her office, this is an area where potential clients are alone and have a few minutes to gather their thoughts. The reinforcement of her credibility in being featured in local magazines is strong. And she repeatedly gets compliments on how nice her bathroom is!

She wants to do it all. We all know brides who think they can make their centerpieces the day of the wedding, place the chair covers, set out their place cards, and organize the entire wedding party the day of their wedding. Few can do this without being overly stressed and utterly exhausted by the end of the night. But the Savvy bride believes she is the one who can do it with ease and grace.

The bottom line is that Savvy brides have a challenging time letting go of control on their wedding days. You may find this to be true just as much in the beginning of the sales process as on the big day. Tailoring your sales and marketing efforts to keep this in mind, therefore, will only benefit you.

She's mindful of quality and budget. Nearly every single Savvy respondent from our focus group said that she didn't believe that she should have to sacrifice quality for less money. A Savvy bride understands that some vendors and items may cost more for the quality she's receiving. But don't take that as an indication you can charge her more. She's also not afraid to shop around to make sure you're not taking advantage of her.

Show her your professionalism. If you find yourself meeting with a Savvy bride, it's time to pull out your most professional demeanor. Your timely and efficient responsiveness and excellent customer service can win her respect quickly (which is what you desire so she doesn't move on to your competition). Try to return her phone calls and e-mails within twenty-four hours, and if you can't, send her a quick reply to let her know you've received her message and will respond within a certain allotted amount of time (in the next day, by the end of the week, etc.). She will appreciate your attention to her needs and will typically wait to receive your response before making a decision, as long as it isn't too long of a wait.

If you don't like talking about yourself, keep in mind that this is the bride whose confidence you need to earn. My Savvy brides have told me over and over again how experience and competence can make all the difference in the vendors they select. She wants to know the awards you've won, the organizations you are a part of, and the community services to which you donate. Make sure to tour her through your office to show her your plaques, or let her browse through magazines you are featured in while you wrap up your phone calls before your meeting. Don't go overboard and talk about it too much, but certainly show her your credibility.

What Not to Do
When interviewing Savvy brides, we found that there are some crucial things to avoid if you want to attract them and achieve the sale.

Don't showcase poor marketing materials. Savvy brides are critical purveyors of vendor marketing. Poorly worded websites or marketing materials are an easy turn-off to this client. Make sure you have plenty of people frequently read over your marketing efforts to ensure that there are no misspellings or grammar issues. And don't underestimate the power of spell check when communicating with her!

In addition to spelling and grammar, the overall look of a website or advertisement can play a big role in portraying your credibility. A homemade ad that features a picture you may think is beautiful is hard to compare to a professionally made one that has a specific sales strategy and a picture shot specifically for the ad. Think about everything from lighting to staging. If you have a wedding coming up that you think is ad worthy, ask the photographer beforehand if you can stage and light a certain moment—or at least tell them what you want so they can keep that in the back of their mind for when the right shot comes their way.

Don't be pushy. Don't be a stereotypical salesperson! Even though she'll appreciate a good offer made, she won't be overly impressed with someone who is e-mailing her every day and keeps telling her that she has the most popular date for next year. For the most part, a Savvy bride won't keep you waiting for long, but she does want the respect of some time to interview all of her prospects.

If you do have other business that is interested in the same date, politely call her or e-mail her personally to let her know that you will hold her date for another forty-eight hours and then you will meet with the other prospects. After that, it is a first-come, first-served basis. In the meantime, if you have another prospect who is ready to book, give the Savvy the option for a first right of refusal. She will appreciate the communication even if she decides not to book you.

The majority of Savvy brides we interviewed said that they feel anxious about handing over the details of their wedding day.

How can you help her feel more at ease?

Don't tell her about everything that went wrong right away. It's rare to have a wedding that goes absolutely according to plan. Timelines are crucial, but it's difficult for things to go off exactly as timed. Speeches go long, buses run late, and people eat slowly. This stuff happens! Just don't take her through every detail of what didn't go according to schedule.

A Savvy bride has trusted you with her most special day. Unless it is an issue that needs her help to be resolved or you think she needs to be aware of it (say it happened behind the scenes), simply make a note of it and move on.

This is exactly what happened to Lynn, a friend of mine. Lynn was a Savvy bride and she was pretty proud of her wedding. She had worked hard, even up until days before when she and her friends noticed the cutest cookies in a magazine that they just had to make for the wedding.

She didn't know this on the day of the wedding, but one small box of about ten place cards went missing. Her grandmother's place card was one of those that wasn't there. When her grandmother went to find her seat, the hotel told her she wasn't allowed into the reception, as there wasn't a card for her.

Fortunately, Lynn's parents intervened and she wasn't made aware of it until after the honeymoon. This was a good thing for her! As a Savvy bride, she would have let something like this bother her (even ever so slightly) and then would have worried about all of the other details. She did want to know, but telling her *after* the wedding about something that couldn't be fixed anyway was a good way for her not to be overly upset and to continue enjoying her day.

More than 90% of Savvy brides said they buy on quality versus budget.

What makes your services or products worth what you charge?

It's no surprise that a Savvy bride has high expectations. These brides can help us hone our own businesses and become better at what we do—both artistically and in business. So when meeting with a Savvy bride, remember:

-   It's okay to brag about yourself a little! Showcase your awards and honors, just don't go overboard.

-   Acknowledge what she already knows. Be impressed by the time and effort she has put into making her wedding her own.

-   Be professional! Show up on time and follow up promptly. Deliver on all of your promises.

-   Showcase professionally created marketing materials. Don't underestimate the power of a proper photo shoot and graphic designer.

-   Be open and honest about what didn't go according to plan, but be mindful of your timing.

My Personal Sales Strategy—Savvy Bride

Honors: What have I been recognized for?

_____

_____

_____

How can I include that in my sales consultation?

_____

_____

_____

Where can I showcase written material in my marketing tools and/or in my office?

_____

_____

_____

Marketing Materials: What marketing materials do I need to create?

_____

_____

_____

Which ones need to be updated?

_____

_____

Do I need to create a photo shoot?

_____

Who can I work with for designing these materials?

_____

_____

What is my budget?

_____

_____

What is my timeline?

_____

_____

Wow: How can I *wow* a Savvy bride during my sales consultation to demonstrate how beneficial it is to work with me?

_____

_____

Am I relaxing? Creative? Organized? How?

_____

_____

Can I meet her somewhere unique or create an experience that allows her to experience these attributes?

_____

_____

Working with a Savvy

This might sound surprising, but working with a Savvy bride can be intimidating. The Savvy bride is constantly on the lookout for something new … something *different*. She can sometimes make you feel as though she is questioning your judgment and expertise.

But what we should understand as vendors working with a Savvy bride is that she is seeking a partner with whom she can brainstorm about these innovative ideas. She wants someone to be able to tell her that things work well in a certain setting, for example, versus in the pages of a magazine.

So your expertise is both wanted and appreciated, but you're also going to have to be able to sit back and listen to her questions and her thoughts. Be open-minded to doing new things. This is not the type of bride who wants to hear, "We usually set the room this way," or "We always take photographs here." These comments will not appeal to her.

She is secure enough and sophisticated enough to shake things up and try something new. And she wants to be confident that you're going to be able to handle the change.

Additional Savvy Bride Tips

- *Head off all issues.* The important thing with a Savvy bride is to never let her discover things on her own in regard to her wedding. If you find out something is happening, let her know (i.e., there is construction being done at the wedding venue during her wedding's timeframe, there's been a change in the photographer's assistant, etc.). She may have questions regarding what to do, so be prepared to address those.

- *Let her know of unusual events.* For example, her venue may be having a special fireworks display or special décor due to the holidays. This can be used as a selling feature to her, and she will be grateful for the helpful hints.

- *Bring out the "big guns."* Savvy brides like to be recognized for the fact that they are an important part of your business. Bring out the manager or the owner to meet her if you really want to impress her and enhance her confidence in your services. If you have the opportunity to schedule a meeting with her when the owner is present, or when the bride can meet the chef in uniform, you will see the impact on her.

Typical Savvy Occupations
- Leadership
- Management
- Entrepreneur

Interview with a Savvy Bride
Q&A with Susan Southerland: Nicole, the Savvy Bride

Nicole's wedding is on September 17, a Saturday afternoon. At the time of my interview with Nicole, she is still midstream in hiring her vendors.

Q: What has worried you most about the planning process?

A: My fiancé and I aren't having any problems coming up with ideas and making decisions, but it's hard to balance what we want with our budget. I don't think our budget is particularly restrictive, but I feel like there's so much give and take we are going to have to do. We reserved our site and photographer early on (and put down deposits) and now I worry that we spent too much on those categories and won't be able to spend as much on others.

Q: What worries you the most about the coming wedding day?
A: I'm a control freak, so I want to make sure I have someone who is the point person on the day of that's not me. I've asked a close friend to be my day-of planner and I totally trust her. I know if I didn't have that set up already that I'd be worried most about that. Other than that, I worry about the stress-level and interactions of everyone else for that day.

Q: What about relinquishing control on the big day?
A: I want to do as much preparation ahead of time that I can so I don't have to worry about too much. As I said before, it was important for me to find someone who I could trust to take over the day of. I don't want to deal with little problems, vendors, or being the director of the event that day.

Q: When you attended bridal shows, what did you look for in a potential vendor?
A: I wanted to see pictures/actual products, idea of prices, and a good personality in the vendor.

Q: What was the deciding factor in which vendors you decided to meet/ interview?
A: Honestly, I was entirely turned off by the whole bridal show process. I went to one when I was recently engaged and attended with my fiancé, mom, and sister. A number of the vendors were very aggressive and one actually made comments about my parents paying for everything. I got very offended because my fiancé and I are working very hard to save up to pay for the majority of our wedding. The experience totally turned me

off to where I didn't pursue *any* of the vendors. I've done a lot of research online.

Q: What did you consider a deciding factor when hiring a vendor?
A: So far, I've used my first interactions as a good way to judge the vendor. I'm big on first impressions and customer service, so I've been taking a lot of notes on how the initial interactions are going with vendors—how I'm being treated on the phone, how responsive vendors are, and how they communicate via e-mail. I don't want to work with anyone who makes me feel like they are doing me a favor when I decide to hire them.

Q: What is one thing that you consider to be a "will not hire" characteristic in a vendor?
A: I will not hire someone who is aggressive, dismissive, exhibits bad customer service, and isn't respectful of my budget. I shouldn't be made to feel bad because I only have a certain amount to spend. I understand that certain vendors may be out of range for particular budgets, but no one should be made to feel guilty because they can't afford something.

Q: What is one thing that a vendor has done during the planning process to make him invaluable to you as a Savvy bride?
A: I'm not too far along in the process and haven't begun working with very many vendors. I have, however, already booked a photographer and was very pleased with the guidance he's already given in the timeline of activities. He made it clear that his expertise is available whenever I needed it, but he wasn't pushy or trying to take control at all. I want someone who is available and is a resource, but also lets me stay in the driver's seat.

Q: What is one thing that your vendors can do to make your experience as a Savvy bride absolutely perfect on the wedding day?
A: Plan everything ahead of time and don't talk to me on my wedding day. That sounds harsh, but I really want to do all the work upfront so everything runs smoothly on my wedding day. If something arises, then the vendors should speak with my day-of coordinator.

Q: What do you consider more important: a vendor who will meet your budget, or a vendor who provides the highest quality service?

A: Both—a vendor who provides the highest quality of service that fits within my budget. No one should have to settle for bad quality, regardless of her budget. I don't believe the two are mutually exclusive.

Chapter 4: The Functional Bride

*H*ave you ever gotten a phone call where the first question out of the bride's mouth is, "How much do you charge?" I have—many times. In previous sales seminars I've gone to, the lecturer has typically expressed that any bride who asks about price first is not worth a vendor's time.

I highly disagree.

For Functional brides, that's the language she's comfortable speaking. This by no means indicates she's cheap. And making this assumption could be the biggest mistake we can make as wedding vendors working with Functional brides. We work in the wedding industry and know what to expect from vendors. She doesn't. Imagine if you were buying your first car and asked the salesperson, "How much does it cost?" before you took it for a test drive. Would he turn you away?

I've worked with Functional brides who have had six-figure weddings, but they all wanted to justify each expense. Regardless of how much they were spending, they wanted to know they were getting the best value for their money. Don't miss out on this lucrative segment of the bridal market because you think discussing the cost of your services somehow diminishes their value.

Functional Strengths

Good financial decision maker. If your Functional bride is the one paying for the wedding, she will definitely be able to make quick financial decisions. However, the initial interview process may not be the time that she decides to sign a contract. She's going to have to seek out someone with whom she's comfortable bringing out her inner artist.

Fair negotiator. The Functional bride will most likely want to negotiate finances with you and will expect you to be able to discuss the financial aspects of your business with her. But just like her Savvy counterpart, she understands that wedding vendors have to make money, so she won't make unreasonable requests.

Uber-organized. Much like our Savvy brides, the Functional bride has exceptional organizational skills. She'll be on top of every detail of her wedding, particularly as relates to the Business side.

Functional Weaknesses

Lacks vision. A Functional bride, like all brides, wants to have a wedding that she perceives as unique among her peers. However, she can't create or express what her wedding should look like.

Doesn't "talk" design. If a Functional bride does have an idea of the look and feel that she wants, she isn't easily able to articulate it. Most likely, she'll provide images from blogs and magazines as references to what she finds appealing.

Her wedding can be cookie-cutter. When it comes to planning her wedding, the Functional bride is more likely to copy photos that she sees rather than putting her personal stamp on it. This isn't necessarily a bad thing … unless she attends another wedding where they have copied that same idea. This may actually be one of her bigger fears.

Selling to the Functional Bride

The Functional Bride is rational, organized, and mindful of her budget. As she deliberates among a sea of wedding vendors, she is looking for a sell that is similar to her bridal personality.

This bride has a logical buy. She can many times base her decision on the facts laid out to her rather than how a vendor or product makes her feel. She wants to know the solid, objective answers in order to make the most rational decision.

She does her research! The Functional Bride loves to "shop around." She carefully analyzes each vendor and may even keep a spreadsheet to represent her research. Don't be afraid if she informs you who she has already met with and who is on her list to meet next. She may have a long list of vendors to meet, but you can be the one she picks if you are patient and responsive.

Not to be taken lightly, prompt follow-up is key to gaining the respect of this bride. She may not provide you with an answer immediately, so be patient while she interviews all of her options. By showing your continued interest in her wedding rather than being put off by her questions over things such as pricing, you can begin to develop a trustworthy relationship (if even only by e-mail!). Don't be surprised if she asks for a contract a month or two after you've met. She can be put off by high-pressure sales situations and doesn't appreciate a vendor telling her that she should book quickly because it is a popular date. You can inform her of another bride interested in her date, but try to give her ample time to make her decision and be there for her along the way.

The Functional bride may also know quite a bit about you before meeting you. Be mindful that she has more than likely scoured your website and has looked over your last ten blog entries. Don't waste time telling her the same things she has already read about you; share new stuff! Talk with her about things such as where you grew up and how that has inspired your business, or any recent conferences you've attended and what you learned about the latest ideas and trends. She'll appreciate the extra effort in going beyond what she already knows.

She talks about money. Don't be disappointed if this consultation doesn't touch much on the "fun" and "pretty" stuff. The Functional bride may not feel comfortable with or know what to say about the creative side of her wedding. She sticks with what's comfortable to her. Many times, this means focusing on budget.

However, even though this bride is sensible about money, it doesn't mean that she fully understands why things for her wedding may cost as much as they do. Be prepared for comments or questions such as: "Why is the cake-cutting fee four dollars per person when we can cut it ourselves?" or "Why does an eight-by-ten-inch print cost twenty-five dollars when I can print it for only five dollars at the local copy store?"

Try not to get annoyed with these questions and instead use them as learning tools for the bride. This is an excellent time to showcase your knowledge of weddings by going into detail of why the price is what it is. Be confident and precise with your answers and don't beat around the bush.

After your consultation, it is of great benefit to provide her a detailed proposal. Every element should be listed out with actual costs, or it should be specifically stated that it is an estimate and will vary depending on final selections. Sending her this in writing can put her at ease, and is great documentation for her files.

She wants value. The Functional bride wants to see value in what she is purchasing, so don't automatically assume she's not the "ideal" client because she is talking about money or asking questions that seem harsh. She's looking for your expertise to show her the reason why. Too many times I hear vendors complain about this type of bride or cringe when they get off the phone with her. However, if you're prepared and confident, this booking can be a great sale.

When putting value on your services, consider the lack of creativity she may face. Explain to her how you can help her achieve a beautiful wedding that is unique to her without going over her budget. If you're a florist, showing her examples of how you can achieve her vision is easy. But what do you do if you're a photographer, an officiant, a stationery company, or a caterer? Here are a few examples:

Photographer: Let her know how you can help her feel at ease while taking pictures. You're experienced at posing brides so that they look their best. Perhaps you can take out your camera and work with her for a few minutes to give her an idea of what working with you would be like.

Officiant: Knowing that the Echo-Boomer generation prides itself on being able to do things "differently," let her know that you can work with her on customizing her vows or bring in special rituals to her ceremony.

Stationery: Ask her who her florist is. Let her know that you can work with the florist to choose invitations that match her overall look.

Caterer: Show her how important food presentation is. If she knows that your food will taste and look extraordinary, she will understand your value.

*Quick Tip: have a calculator handy!

Vendors who are prepared with this small detail can make a big difference in the eyes of this bride.

She negotiates. It's important to be prepared for negotiation with a Functional bride. She will probably do this with each vendor and may even do it for a living. She's not afraid to ask for a good deal, and feels satisfied when a vendor demonstrates flexibility. I often hear vendors say that they won't discount their prices. I don't discourage or promote this practice; I only recommend that you keep in mind that inflexibility in pricing may deter this type of bride.

When negotiating with a Functional bride, pricing is typically top of mind. Add-ons may be an option, but consider providing a discount if possible. However, don't be too quick to produce an answer. Take your time and step into your office for a moment to "look at things" or tell her you will look at numbers that evening and will see what you can do for her. This brief "time to think" can give you a moment to gather your thoughts on what is best for your business, and shows her you are seriously considering her negotiation.

She wants to know what has worked and what hasn't. We all have wedding stories—for good and bad. The Functional bride wants to know about them! Share with her what went well at weddings (such as tents without walls due to your region's weather, or candles only after 6:00 PM if an outdoor ceremony) and tell her about instances that were challenging (such as maitre d' seating for five hundred people, or a horse and carriage ride down a busy road). She will appreciate knowing all of the facts and the honesty you provide. And it may even get a few laughs!

The Functional bride also likes to see pictures of what has been done in the past. Don't overwhelm her with books and books of previous weddings, but do show her a good number of varied options. It can be difficult for her to explain what she likes, so showing her pictures can be a helpful tool for her to describe her vision. This is also a great way for you to sell options that you prefer, items you already have, and programs that you know work well.

In return, ask her what she has seen at weddings she has attended that she liked. Does she remember anything that didn't go well or that she didn't care for? This will give you insight into what style and preferences she has as well.

She wants to know what other clients think. The power of testimonials for a Functional bride can be huge. She's interested in hearing of your previous clients' experiences with you and if there were any issues.

Testimonials can be part of your website, electronic brochures, and print materials. However, ask her if she would like a list of clients she can call or e-mail to ask about their experiences with you. Take the initiative to provide her with this at your sales consultation. Whether she takes you up on it or not, it distinguishes your credibility.

Don't be afraid to ask past couples for their testimonials and go beyond just the bride. Many times, having a quote from the groom, a parent, or a guest can make just as big of an impact.

> *Where can brides currently see your testimonials?*
>
> *Are they placed throughout your website?*
>
> *Are they on your collateral?*

What Not to Do

Don't be inflexible. We know that the Functional bride is not afraid to negotiate. She may even expect it from each of her vendors. I've had a Functional bride tell me she wouldn't book any vendors that wouldn't negotiate with her.

Remember that negotiation can be flexible in a variety of ways. Offering discounted pricing for the most popular Saturday in a season may not be a feasible option. But hiring a contractor to assist her on your behalf or presenting the possibility of an alternate date may allow your pricing to adjust slightly. Don't feel that you have to give in, but make sure that you showcase your flexibility by providing other options.

Don't be nonresponsive. Functional brides are prompt and they expect you to be, too. They carefully manage their time and desire the same respect from their vendors. Poor responsiveness can be interpreted as a lack of organization—and we know how organized a Functional bride likes to be!

If you are unable to respond within twenty-four hours, have an associate reach out or send her a brief note letting her know when to expect your response. She'll appreciate you acknowledging her needs.

Don't be unorganized. Details, details, details! The Functional bride loves details—but in the business side of things. She takes note of your grammar, punctuation, and certainly the spelling of her name.

Make sure to double-check your e-mails or any communication with a Functional bride prior to sending. Your flawlessness may not get you all of the business, but it can definitely help ensure that you don't lose business over it.

The Functional bride will be prepared when she comes to meet with you, so take time beforehand to prepare to meet with her as well. It will show! Don't fly in from a previous meeting where papers are strewn around and you're trying to find your glasses while the phone is ringing off the hook. Take a moment to gather yourself, organize your office area, forward your phone, and have your notebook ready.

And when you finally do meet with her, keep in mind these few tips:

- Share new information about yourself.

- Don't be afraid to talk costs and budget.

- Be open to negotiating and take time to make sure it is right for your business.

- Explain efficiently and effectively why things cost what they do with your company.

- Show what has worked well in the past.

- Use proper grammar, punctuation, and spell her name correctly!

- Provide her with a list of past clients she can call for testimonials.

- Be patient while she makes her decisions, yet assertive on follow-up e-mails and phone calls to check in regularly.

My Personal Sales Strategy—Functional Bride

Pricing: Why are my services or products priced the way they are?

_____

_____

_____

What is the value to the client?

_____

_____

_____

Why am I, or my product, worth it?

_____

_____

Testimonials: Where can I put testimonials and is it time for new ones?

_____

_____

_____

Do I have a good variety from people other than just brides?

_____

Negotiation: What three things am I willing to negotiate? (Price? Add-ons? Booking incentives?)

_____

_____

_____

Previous Work: How is my previous work displayed?

_____

_____

_____

How do I discuss it in my sales consultations?

_____

_____

_____

How else can I talk about what has worked well in the past?

_____

_____

_____

Working with Functional Brides

For most of us working in weddings, which is by and large a highly creative industry, the Functional bride hits us squarely where we are most insecure. As a well-rounded wedding vendor, you need to know your cost of business. You should have a good understanding of why things related to your business cost what they do, and you'll need to demonstrate to your Functional brides why you charge what you do. There is a value in being the most creative, the most efficient, the most cost-effective, or the most well-known vendor in your category. You need to be able to quantify those values to effectively work with your Functional brides.

Functional brides need sensory representations of your business. If you're a photographer or videographer, for example, be able to show her photos or video clips of her wedding location and show her where some of your more creative or beautiful shots were taken. If you're a florist, present her photos of arrangements in the colors she likes, or pull some flowers out of the cooler for her to touch and study and smell. Music vendors can play samples of their music, cake and banquet vendors can offer samples to taste, and stationery vendors can present her with samples that fit her color choices and personal style.

Again, it is important as vendors that we know our cost of business so that we know where there is room to negotiate. A Functional bride will work outside the box, so if she has a particular spending goal in mind for your services, she will break apart what you normally do and tailor it to what she can spend. It's helpful to present the Functional bride with an editable spreadsheet outlining your service options so that she can work with it to get everything within her budget. The more hands-on a Functional bride can be, the more comfortable she will be.

Additional Functional Bride Tips
- *Don't mistake her for "cheap."* Very often I'll hear sales seminars where they say that if all a bride discusses with you is price, price, price, they'll be too cheap to be worth your while. In fact, for some brides, it's the only way they know how to begin a conversation. As a vendor, you'll need to identify this and learn how to guide the conversation to beyond just price. Stress value and you'll go far toward securing her business.

- *Consider an "interactive" proposal.* The first step after consulting with a bride is going to be sending out an effective proposal. With Functional brides, having a proposal that they can interact with and possibly even make changes to will have the most success.

Typical Functional Occupations
- Accountant
- Attorney
- Engineer
- Scientist

Interview with a Functional Bride
Q&A with Susan Southerland: Mandy, the Functional Bride

Mandy's wedding is on January 4, a Tuesday afternoon. At the time of this interview, she is about halfway done selecting her vendors. She began her wedding planning nearly eighteen months before the big day. Her approach to hiring her vendors has been methodical and carefully planned.

Q: What has worried you most about the planning process?
A: What *hasn't* worried me should be the question. I guess if I had to narrow it down though, it would be whether or not I will be able to stay within my budget. I would also have to include the fact that I may not be able to meet with all the vendors I book since I am planning from a different state.

Q: What worries you the most about the coming wedding day?
A: Whether or not everything will flow together nicely and if my guests will be happy.

Q: How do you feel about relinquishing control on the big day?
A: This is going to be very hard for me. I am definitely the type that likes to do everything myself and I have a difficult time letting people do things for me even if I am 100 percent certain they will do the job much better than I ever could. I guess I just like to see things for myself before I can breathe easy. Hopefully I will be too preoccupied with getting ready myself and with my emotions in general that I will just accept the fact that I can't be everywhere.

Q: When/If you attended bridal shows, what did you look for in a potential vendor?

A: I like vendors with a lot of samples or pictures available and I like when they have a lot of references that I can contact.

Q: What was the deciding factor in which vendors you decided to meet/ interview?

A: Since I am planning our day from another state, I have relied almost entirely on references from other brides who have had weddings in the same area and from my wedding planner. Without these people, I would have vetoed the distance wedding idea a long time ago.

Q: What did you consider a deciding factor when hiring a vendor?

A: Cost, quality, and references. If a vendor was in our price range, we would then look at the quality of their samples and I needed to have heard plenty of good words from other brides, too, before really considering them at all. If our wedding was near where we live, I wouldn't need quite so many references; however, I would still want to hear a few before I would book a vendor.

Q: What is one thing that you consider to be a "will not hire" characteristic in a vendor?

A: A vendor who doesn't care to get back to me when I call or e-mail her, or someone who doesn't want to work with me at all to customize her packages to better suit my needs. Our wedding day is *not* the same as everyone else's; therefore, I may not require the exact same package as the brides who came before me.

Q: What is one thing that a vendor has done during the planning process to make him invaluable to your particular planning personality?

A: Being available to answer all of the random questions that I think of during the week. It's a relief when a vendor takes the time to read my e-mails and answer my questions when I have them and can sense when I need some direction and ideas about all aspects of the wedding.

Q: What is one thing that your vendors can do to make your experience as a Functional bride absolutely perfect on the wedding day?

A: It helps when a vendor can offer me suggestions (without being pushy) on what looks good together and what works well. They are the professionals and I hired them because I value their opinions and most likely can use their guidance in their certain areas of expertise. With that being said, I still want to make sure that our personalities are incorporated into these details as well.

Q: What do you consider more important: a vendor who will meet your budget, or a vendor who provides the highest quality service?

A: I would have to say that our budget is most important; however, quality should not be lacking. A vendor should be able to provide quality service at all different budget levels. If I chose the lowest menu package from a reception venue, and there is pizza on that menu, I expect that pizza to be an *excellent* pizza.

Chapter 5: The Visionary Bride

*H*ave you ever asked a bride to describe the vision she has for her wedding day and the answer is fifteen minutes long? Has a bride gone into so much artistic detail that you wonder how she came up with everything? If so, you were probably working with a Visionary bride.

A telling characteristic of a Visionary bride is that she's very concerned with having her vision met. There's very little room for error! One of my most powerful stories that I use to convey this point when I'm speaking involves truly one of the most beautiful weddings that I've ever done.

My Visionary bride, Sierra, had very accommodating parents, and she was very used to getting what she wanted. Her wedding day was certainly no exception. I worked very closely with her mother to create exactly the wedding Sierra always envisioned.

One of the things that Sierra wanted was royal banquet seating at her reception, which resulted in large, long tables set for forty or fifty guests. It was also very important to her that each guest sit in a specific location. Thus, not only did we have assigned tables, but we had assigned seats for 250 guests. Her mother worked for hours on a chart for my staff and me to follow when laying out the seating cards. It took us quite a bit of time to do, but after checking it three or four times, we were quite certain that everyone was in his and her proper place.

The ceremony came and went perfectly and the guests enjoyed a beautiful cocktail hour while Sierra and her new husband were getting photos taken. Then it came time for the guests to be seated, the wedding party to be introduced, and the bride and groom to have the first dance.

The music cued up and the wedding party was introduced without incident. Next, Sierra and her husband were introduced with much fanfare and we opened the ballroom doors. I watched as they walked to the dance floor and began their first dance.

Then I noticed that this Visionary bride had an odd (if not slightly perturbed) look on her face, and I continued to watch as they completed their dance. She walked up to her table, which already had forty guests seated at it, planted her feet and crossed her arms and loudly declared that nothing else was going to take place until the people on the right side of the table took their glasses and switched places with the people on the left side of the table.

Evidently, Sierra's mother had reversed the order in which her guests were to be seated at this particular table. Fortunately for all, the guests did exactly as they were ordered and the reception continued without further incident.

This Visionary bride's sister later came up behind me and whispered in my ear, "At least she didn't start crying."

Visionary Strengths
Highly creative. The Visionary bride will bring special touches and fun, personal elements into the look of her wedding. I recently worked with a bride who didn't want to spend a lot of money on menu cards, so she printed her own and added her own embellishments by gluing rhinestones to them. This creative trait should prompt vendors to offer services that allow the Visionary to exercise her abilities. Photographers, for example, can offer albums that a bride can lay out and then the photographer can print.

Also, working with Visionaries almost always means you will end up with a beautiful example of your work for portfolios and demonstration purposes.

Great fashion and style sense. The Visionary bride may wear the latest styles and colors, piecing together the perfect outfit for every meeting. On her wedding day, everything will look just as well balanced. The Art element of the wedding will be well put together. If you as a vendor lean more toward the business side of planning, she'll help you create some beautiful work that you might not otherwise have done.

Open to new ideas. The Visionary bride is going to be excellent at collaboration when it comes to the Art side of her wedding. If you're also a Visionary, she may help give you a new and exciting perspective to infuse in your work.

Media-savvy. Visionary brides are the brides who pore over wedding blogs and magazines. She's also very often an effective do-it-yourselfer. She's very conceptual and can usually more easily grasp your ideas without a lot of tangible photos and samples.

Visionary Weaknesses

Not money-minded. The Visionary bride will come up with all kinds of fantastic and creative ideas and can be easily sold on your ideas as well. However, she doesn't understand that she may be overspending. She has no real concept of what she can or can't afford. It may take her time to sign a contract because she may have to seek advice from others when it comes to her spending. On the other hand, she may just recklessly decide to contract for services and then realize later she has overspent, meaning she'll have to change things up to meet her budget.

She's disorganized. Organization is definitely not in the Visionary bride's typical personality spectrum. She may forget to meet deadlines and will need some hand-holding to ensure she completes those business tasks you need her to do.

She can have an artistic temperament. The picture we all have in our heads about the temperamental artist definitely holds true for the Visionary bride. She may have a set image in her mind of how things will look and how things are meant to be on her wedding day, and as my "cautionary tale" above reminds you, if it doesn't go that way, she's liable to let that temperament get the better of her.

Selling to the Visionary Bride

The Visionary bride loves creativity and enjoys exploring the endless possibilities on how to make her wedding unique and personal. She may, at times, need to be kept on track, but in the end she can be a lot of fun and a great addition to your portfolio.

This type of bride typically buys on emotion. If someone or something makes her feel good, excited, or awed, she has a higher tendency to purchase. If it doesn't feel right, why would she go for it? Her wedding day is about *wow*ing not only her guests, but also herself.

She wants her senses to ignite. The Visionary bride wants to see it, feel it, hear it, smell it, and taste it. The more she can experience her wedding before it happens, the better!

We may feel that the flower coolers holding typical red roses for an anniversary delivery are mundane, or that the dinner rolls at each place setting are boring, but to the Visionary bride, these are elements she relishes. She loves to look in the cooler and take in the colors and scents. She enjoys listening to the new mix you just downloaded. And she may even ask if their initials can be marked into the dinner roll butter! No detail is too small, and she's determined to keep it that way.

Visionary brides see things "outside of the box," so consider that when you're selling to her. Instead of showing her wedding album after wedding album, you may choose to let her browse while you take a few head shots of her (or, let's say, some shots of a faux cake or dress) in your studio and then show her your creative process of how you artistically manipulate it. Or let her browse through your racks of fabrics, encouraging her to note the feel and look of each one. And she'll love a taste of whatever the chefs are cooking up at the moment!

She needs guidance on budget. The Visionary bride can sometimes be a tricky sale. Many times, a Visionary gushes over everything she wants during her consultation meeting. The more ideas you throw out, the more she wants them. By the time she's left, you have dollar signs in your eyes and are starting to think what magazine you're going to submit this wedding to for publication. However, be mindful that she may not be anticipating what your pricing will be with everything she wants, or she may not even know what her budget is. These are the brides that come back and cut half of the items you so excitedly discussed with your team.

It's important not to focus too much on numbers with a Visionary bride, but do be honest and upfront. Take her ideas and price them out accordingly, and let her know before she signs what the cost will be (or a good estimate) and when payments are due.

She can sometimes forget. Most importantly: document, document, document! The Visionary bride is not out to take you for a ride, but she may not have the organization in place to remember what you quoted her. You have to do that for her. I recommend putting everything that was discussed in writing and e-mailing it to her. Or encourage her to e-mail you any questions so you can both keep good records. Keep a correspondence log for any phone calls and make sure to note any pricing that was discussed. You may find that her beautiful (and endless) ideas come with quite a bit of follow-up, and it's important that everything is documented accordingly.

To ensure your payments are received in a timely manner, try to e-mail her a reminder at least one week prior to your payment due date. Don't be surprised if your contract or deposits don't arrive on the scheduled date, but kindly follow up to remind her.

She may make her decisions quickly. The Visionary bride tends to be an emotional buyer. She loves how things make her feel and can make a quick decision in order to get what she wants. This can be a swift and easy contract if you are prepared!

With all of the pretty colors, the outstanding pictures, the energetic dance songs, and the delicious food, the Visionary bride can't resist. Unlike the Functional bride who analyzes and researches, Visionaries book vendors who excite their imaginations and give them a good vibe. They can fall in love with you on the spot and not care how much it will cost—your talent is worth it!

If you notice this happening, don't be afraid to ask for the sale on the spot. She won't want anyone else to book you on her wedding day, so she may be willing to provide you a deposit right then and there, even if she has another appointment scheduled after you. If you're able to sign her right away, consider whether you have been up-front about all costs and remember to make note of it in your contract or file notes and follow up with an e-mail. Also, be sure to highlight your cancellation policy just in case she changes her mind when she gets home.

She wants to be heard. Visionary brides have been dreaming of this day for as long as they can remember. They can't get enough ideas and love sharing theirs with everyone. It's crucial to take time to listen to this bride. Ask her open-ended questions that allow her creativity to flow and for her to express everything she has always wanted.

A Visionary can have great stories of what her wedding day will be like, and she can go on for quite some time. Don't cut her off or rush her. Let her enjoy this time of talking with someone who appreciates her creative touches and may even have more ideas for her!

The Visionary bride won't necessarily mind if your office is a tad messy (but please, no disasters), and she may run a little late. Think about how you can showcase your creative side when you meet with her and play into that.

What Not to Do

Don't assume she has a large budget. The Visionary bride has ideas galore and talks about them as though she can afford them all. We've all experienced what it's like once we learn what the real budget is, though. It's important to know that not every Visionary has an endless budget, even though it may initially seem like it. Make sure you take a moment to ask what her budget is, and give her options in different price ranges so she can select something beautiful, but feasible.

Don't rush her. Expressing her feelings and doodling about her dreams are things the Visionary bride loves to do. Yes, this appointment may run an hour longer than a Savvy or Functional bride's, but listening to her desires and vision is the number-one thing to do when first meeting with a Visionary. Try not to get antsy if your meeting runs long, and make sure she feels that she has expressed all of her wants to you before you wrap up.

Don't dismiss deadlines. Have you ever had a consultation with a bride where it seemed you knew the entire look and feel of her entire wedding and she hadn't even signed a contract yet? It's easy to get so involved with the beautiful, fun things about planning a wedding with a Visionary bride that we forget to collect contracts and payments on time. It's essential that you stick to a strict timeline with a Visionary bride and gently remind her of approaching deadlines. Not only is this helpful with your own accounting, but other vendors will also appreciate your follow-up.

When meeting with a Visionary bride, remember:

- Don't rush her. Listen attentively and let her speak. Ask her how things make her feel.

- Have patience and don't be in a hurry.

- Be mindful of her ideas, but don't forget to discuss costs.

- Document everything! Follow up with an e-mail recap and save it in your records.

- Go ahead! If you feel it's right, ask for the sale on the spot!

My Personal Sales Strategy—Visionary Bride

Documentation: How do I currently document all communication?

_____

_____

What is my file system like (printed and electronic)?

_____

_____

What improvements do I need to make?

_____

_____

Experience: How creative is my sales consultation? Why?

_____

_____

What can I do to show her or have her experience uniqueness in my company?

_____

_____

What questions can I ask that will allow her to dream big?

_____

_____

What projects can I give her to do at home (if she's interested) in order to keep her engaged?

_____

_____

Immediate Purchase: What can I offer as an incentive for her to book on the spot or within twenty-four hours?

_____

_____

Budget: How can I cautiously discuss budget without upsetting her dreams?

_____

_____

How can I involve her in DIY projects that might help her stay within her budget while allowing me to do the highly creative part?

_____

_____

Working with Visionary Brides

When working with a Visionary bride, your "business advisor" skills will have to be put into play. She's going to need your guidance on how and what she can spend for your services. Allow her to sit and paint you a picture through your conversation of what she envisions for her wedding, but be sure to bring her back to how she can budget to afford it. You need to convey to her that you want her to achieve her vision and provide everything she wants, but you need to be guided by how much she is able to afford.

This may seem counterintuitive for a good salesperson; however, if she doesn't have sufficient funds to get everything in her vision, you may find yourself putting a lot of work into her wedding and then toward the end of the planning process having to redo everything to cut it back to what she can afford.

If she has a significant budget for your services, demonstrating to the Visionary bride that you're mindful of what she is spending will help gain her trust. When you have that trust established, you'll be able to upsell her for additional services.

You will have to help keep her organized. Make sure you give her ample notice of any payment deadlines as well as paperwork that is due prior to the wedding, because she will most likely not remember these on her own. And from a future sales and marketing standpoint, if you want to be able to use the Visionary bride's wedding in your future sales and marketing efforts, make sure to ask her for a letter of reference or even take dictation over the phone with her reference, as she is most likely not going to remember to do it on her own.

Additional Visionary Bride Tips
- Don't show her a dirty room (messy is one thing, but filthy is quite another!)
- Make sure to get paid in full in advance
- Detail everything on the Banquet Event Order (BEO)
- If you want a testimonial from her, write down a quote

Typical Visionary Occupations
- Graphic Artists
- Designers
- Photographers
- Performers

Interview with a Visionary Bride
Q&A with Susan Southerland: Crystal, the Visionary Bride

Note to the reader: We requested many Visionary interviews, but didn't receive many responses. This supported our findings that Visionaries are not very good at remitting their responses when requested. Nevertheless, we dug down and managed to find the perfect Visionary to participate in this project!

Crystal's wedding was on April 10, a Sunday afternoon. At the time of my interview with Crystal, her planning as well as her wedding had already taken place.

Q: What worried you most about the planning process?
A: That it would not just be about *my* vision and *my* ideas. My fiancé also had very specific ideas about certain things, and I felt it was important that our celebration carry his stamp as well as mine.

Q: What worried you the most about the wedding day as it approached?

A: That the gardens we were using wouldn't be blooming and filled in (they were), and I was terrified that no one would show up (they did).

Q: How did you feel about relinquishing control on the big day?

A: I know I'm a super-minority here, but because of the kind of wedding we had, and how we put it together, it was *very* easy to hand it over to friends and family and let myself enjoy the day.

Q: When/If you attended bridal shows, what did you look for in a potential vendor?

A: I looked for vendors that were real people … small booths with little traffic. Huge crowds around the booth? Not for me. Sweepstakes? No, thank you. I prefer to support small, local businesses, and I found much of the wedding show hype offensive.

Q: What was the deciding factor in which vendors you decided to meet/interview?

A: Location. It was very important to me to shop locally as much as possible.

Q: What did you consider a deciding factor when hiring a vendor?

A: Whether or not they had what I wanted, pricing (of course), and communication. I can't work with a vendor if I can't be sure that they understand me, and vice versa.

Q: What was one thing that you considered a "will not hire" characteristic in a vendor?

A: Indifference to my vision. I had a florist tell me that he's "not so much into greenery" when I asked for a bouquet that included herbs, and that I should "have a cousin you don't care about do the centerpieces during the ceremony." Clearly, he didn't share my enthusiasm for what I was doing.

Q: What is one thing that a vendor did during the planning process to make him invaluable to you as a Visionary bride?

A: Offering ideas that fit within my budget and helping me to refine my vision by coming up with creative solutions to challenging situations.

Q: What is one thing that your vendors did for you as a Visionary bride to make your experience absolutely perfect on the wedding day?
A: They got on board and were enthusiastic! I wanted to know that they were as invested in my event as I was and would make it happen without being monitored.

Q: What did you consider more important: a vendor who met your budget, or a vendor who provided the highest quality service?
A: I wouldn't settle for less than both!

Chapter 6: The Bewildered Bride

*O*ne thing that Bewildered brides have in common is that they tend to be extremely sweet and incredibly eager to please. In that respect, this makes working with them absolutely delightful. At the same time, this people-pleasing characteristic can make planning a wedding absolutely excruciating!

A perfect example of this is a Bewildered bride, Ava, with whom I worked very closely in selecting the color scheme for her wedding. Ava adored pastel colors. The soft tones were exactly what she envisioned for her spring wedding. We worked for hours selecting photos for an inspiration board, and we finally put all of the pieces together; it was absolutely exquisite. Ava was extremely proud and excited with what we had come up with, and she couldn't wait to share her ideas with her friends.

Upon sharing her inspiration board with her maid of honor, her maid of honor declared that it looked like a gigantic Easter egg basket. Ava was devastated. I spent hours on the phone with her bolstering her confidence and reminding her about how excited she was about the work we had done and the color scheme we had come up with, and that her wedding was supposed to be a true reflection of her and her groom. I carefully emphasized that the opinions of others truly had no place in her final decision-making process.

Ava finally relaxed and once again became excited about the decision she had made. But, as with all Bewildered brides, the months leading up to her wedding were filled with the question of "Did I do the right thing?"

Bewildered Strengths

A blank canvas. A Bewildered bride is typically overwhelmed by the entire planning process. Financially, she doesn't know where she needs to be, and she has no concept of the artistic side of planning, either. Even if she does have any ideas, she's typically too overwhelmed to implement them. However, this means that a Bewildered bride truly has an open mind regarding anything and everything a vendor has to say to her.

People pleaser. She's going to be eager to make her vendors happy, so she should be very pleasant to work with. It should be an enjoyable planning process, as long as she isn't getting overwhelmed.

Flexible. Unlike our other planning personalities, the Bewildered bride isn't tied into one set concept for her wedding. She'll be adaptable when it comes to every element of her wedding, from the budget to the vision. For example, a Bewildered bride planning an outdoor wedding who has to move it inside because of weather is more likely to go with the flow than any other type of bride, as long as you show her that everything is in control and going to be okay.

Bewildered Weaknesses

Indecisive. Because a Bewildered bride is so open to thoughts and ideas of other people, remember that you will not be her only influencing factor. Despite the effort that you put forth in helping her make her decisions, it may take only a moment for someone else to obliterate all of the work that you've done.

Hypercommunicative. Over the years, I've found that my Bewildered brides take up the majority of my time. A Bewildered bride will constantly call and e-mail for reassurance, and if one of her friends or relatives shakes her confidence in any of her decisions about your category of services, you will definitely find yourself dedicating a great deal of time reestablishing her confidence in her decisions.

Busy, busy, busy. When it comes to planning her wedding, the Bewildered bride's attention is rather scattered. She's focused on more than just wedding planning ... work, family, etc. Sometimes these preoccupations are genuine distractions, and sometimes they're just convenient ways for her to avoid tasks she can't seem to focus on.

People pleaser. What is a strength for the Bewildered bride is also a weakness. Her eagerness to make everybody happy can cause her to do things that make the bride herself unhappy.

Selling to the Bewildered Bride

Due to the reasons outlined above, the Bewildered bride can struggle with both the Art and the Business side of planning her wedding. Many Bewildered brides are busy with careers and/or family and don't have the time or the passion that other brides do to participate in the planning process.

Bewildereds have a tendency to buy based on others' opinions as well as the ease of working with a certain vendor or company. She may not have the time, desire, or knowledge-base to interview a variety of vendors, or she just may not know who to pick without the help of someone else's input.

She doesn't know where to begin or what to ask. As I've previously mentioned, I've often heard vendors state that if the first question a bride asks is, "How much do you charge?" they aren't worth pursuing. The fact is, this is a very valid question for a bride to ask us, and might be the only one that a Bewildered bride thinks to ask. I encourage you to be open-minded when a bride does ask this question. It may be because she has no idea what else to ask!

It's important to have patience with a Bewildered bride. She may provide one-word answers to many of your questions, and at times, may not even know what to answer. She can sometimes hem and haw about when she's getting married, where she's getting married, and how many people will attend. She just doesn't know and hasn't made up her mind!

Try to gently guide a Bewildered bride through your sales consultation. Unlike other bridal personalities such as the Savvy, who may dominate and control the consultation, a Bewildered bride is looking to you to help her along.

She gets overwhelmed easily. If you've ever had a bride with a glazed-over look in her eyes telling you that you've overdone it with details, you could easily have been talking with a Bewildered bride. Too many ideas or details at once can put her in a panic. She could either be completely disengaged and not interested in the details, or she could be worried that she hasn't thought of any of it and now she might be behind.

When consulting with a Bewildered bride, stick to easy, straightforward questions. It's not necessary to talk details, so be mindful of giving out too much information. If she doesn't know her colors, don't start throwing out colors with names like "tangerine" or "evergreen." Keep it simple in the beginning, opting for the more common "orange" or "green." As the planning gets more involved, the smaller details such as the tones or hues of a color can be discussed.

She's influenced by others. One way to spot a Bewildered bride is that many times she arrives with an entourage, or someone in her peer group may call on her behalf. Because decisions can be difficult for her to make, she relies on others to help her make the "right" ones.

My Personal Sales Strategy—Bewildered Bride

People Pleaser: How do I cater to others in her circle of influence? Her parents? Her friends?

_____

_____

How can I sell more to her circle of influence?

_____

_____

Organization: What is my follow-up process?

_____

_____

How can I gently guide this bride throughout her planning?

_____

_____

Working with Bewildered Brides

Once again, working with a Bewildered bride requires patience and understanding. Our efforts with her will definitely be more time-consuming than with any other planning personality. If you have a nurturing personality, working with a Bewildered bride can be very gratifying, as if she is happy, she will be forever grateful.

For those of us who are good decision makers, we may at times feel as though we're being manipulated by the Bewildered bride. It can be difficult to understand how a person can agonize over every decision. However, if we understand this about the Bewildered bride going into the planning process with her, this can help relieve some of our frustration.

I've found that it's very important to put everything in writing when working with a Bewildered bride. Because she's so scattered and she takes in so many ideas, it's easy for everyone to be confused as to what the final decisions actually were. Even if I have a phone conversation with a Bewildered bride, I like to follow it up with a summary e-mail, and I typically ask her a question at the end of the e-mail, which forces her to reply to me so that I have a record that she has read the e-mail. This can come in very handy if there are any misunderstandings later.

"After learning about the Bewildered bride during one of Susan's presentations, I immediately identified some of my most challenging weddings as being those with this bride. I have found that even though I am their photographer, I many times find myself helping unwrap the favors or helping her with her dress, as there is no clear structure of the day and of who is doing what. I now encourage my Bewildered brides to hire a coordinator when possible."—Kim Nordurft, photographer, Kim Nordurft Photography

A bit surprisingly, Bewildered brides may have strong abilities in either the Business or Art side of planning. However, they are often too busy or too scattered to follow through with their ideas. Vendors must take advantage of the moments where a Bewildered is focused and really communicating.

I also have a suggestion if the Bewildered bride is not the financial decision maker. Be sure to invite the person responsible for handling those matters to all key appointments where contracts are being signed and payments are being made. Having that person present at contract signings and key decision-making meetings will save you from having to repeat the meeting at a later time to justify the expenses or the decisions.

Something that we as vendors really need to keep in mind when working with Bewildered brides is that their openness to everything puts us in a position of great responsibility. All of the suggestions we make will be taken very seriously by this bride, and we're truly in the position of shaping what she is going to be spending and what her wedding is going to look like. Treat this responsibility with sincere respect. This is definitely a time when we should go beyond being just super salespeople to being more conscientious and, well, *human*.

Additional Bewildered Bride Tips
- Make sure she signs off on everything!
- Provide her reminders via e-mail and phone every few days or weeks until her task is completed.
- Be mindful of her circle of influence and sell to them just as much as to her.

Typical Bewildered Occupations
- All types

Interview with a Bewildered Bride
Q&A with Susan Southerland: Kimberley, the Bewildered Bride

Kim's destination wedding is on May 13, a Thursday afternoon. At the time of my interview with Kimberley, she is entirely done hiring her vendors; most of them have been booked through a customized wedding package offered by her venue and their preferred coordinators.

Q: What has worried you most about the planning process?
A: We currently live in Yellowknife, Northwest Territories, Canada, and wanted to get married in Orlando, Florida. I was very worried that although we weren't planning a huge wedding, we still wouldn't be able to get quite what we wanted on our day. Thanks to our coordinator, I believe things will turn out very lovely and just what we always wanted.

Q: What worries you the most about the coming wedding day?

A: I am actually not too worried at all. We planned a very small, intimate ceremony and quiet dinner so I am not worried that things can go wrong. I honestly just want to enjoy the day and be as easy-going as I can be. If an issue comes up, I want to be able to laugh it off and look back on the day and just say that we had a great wedding day.

Q: What about relinquishing control on the big day?

A: I am actually quite happy about it! I think I want to be as relaxed as I can be that day, so someone else watching and coordinating things eases my mind.

Q: When you attended bridal shows, what did you look for in a potential vendor?

A: I did not attend bridal shows; however, if I had the opportunity, I think I would just want to ensure they were willing to work with what we wanted. For example, we didn't want a four-course meal, so if a vendor could not work within our limitations, then it wouldn't work at all.

Q: What did you consider a deciding factor when hiring a vendor?

A: I really trusted our ceremony coordinator; she knew what we wanted and had worked with many vendors before, so I had to just trust that everything would be okay. With planning so far away, I think it is very important to get a planner that you trust, and let them run with it.

Q: What is one thing that you consider to be a "will not hire" characteristic in a vendor?

A: I think it is really important for vendors to understand that everyone is different. We received a lot of "package" info, which was great, but not at all what we were wanting (big dinners, DJs, etc). Vendors sometimes have to "think outside the box" when they get a client that may not want it all. It was also very important to me that although we weren't having a huge wedding, it was still very special, and they treat it as such.

Q: What is one thing that a vendor has done during the planning process to make him invaluable to you as a Bewildered bride?

A: It's important for vendors to get the idea from the couple of what they are looking for, but also provide alternatives and other suggestions. For me, just providing answers like "yes" or "no" didn't cut it. I needed and wanted more info back so we could then decide on things as opposed to having to research a thought all over again. I was just too busy with my work to spend a lot of time on researching.

Q: What is one thing that your vendors can do to make your experience as a Bewildered bride absolutely perfect on the wedding day?

A: I think it is most important to feel supported and that they have done and will do everything that has been agreed upon. If there are any questions, the vendor should have brought them up days prior, and not the day of.

Q: What do you consider more important: a vendor who will meet your budget, or a vendor who provides the highest quality service?

A: I think the vendor that provides the highest quality of service. As the old saying goes, "You get what you pay for," so if you are really budget conscious, then you have to let go of some of the quality, unfortunately. Vendors should be able to supply a nice balance, however; if not, quality is more important.

Chapter 7: Identifying and Discovering

Now that you have an understanding of each bridal personality, how do you identify the personality of a bride when she contacts you?

We have two primary ways of identifying a bride's personality. The first, our personality quiz, is fun for brides to take on their own. It makes them feel more like they are a part of the process of their own discovery. The second, discovered by you and not openly discussed, can be used each time you talk with a bride as long as you are mindful of what you are analyzing.

Personality Quiz

The easiest and most ideal way to identify a bride's personality is by having her take the quiz (appendix A) my team and I developed. It can be found at <u>www</u> <u>.susansoutherland.com</u> and can also be printed out for vendors to bring along to appointments for the brides to take. It can actually be quite fun to hand this to a bride while she's waiting for her appointment—it's an easy and quick tool that provides a plethora of information! And a bride typically appreciates the fact that you're making an effort to tailor your services to best suit her.

This quiz is designed to get brides thinking of how they respond in planning situations outside of their weddings and in everyday life. We look for things such as what role they play in planning activities and even how they shop at the mall. It's a way for us to look into their daily lives and see any trends that emerge in regard to planning and selling.

To give you an idea what to expect, here are a few of the questions from the quiz:

If you were a volunteer on a party-planning committee, what job would you most want to have?

a) I would be president! I like to oversee all aspects of the party and have a good grasp on budgeting, decorating, and delegating.

b) I would be responsible for operations. I enjoy researching things such as location, date, and vendors. And I'll make sure we stay within our budget!

c) I would lead the creative efforts. My passion lies in selecting a theme and designing the overall look. My ideas are endless!

d) I prefer to help out wherever the team needs me. In planning a party, I just prefer to receive direction from those that are planning it—I'm too busy to plan a party right now!

When attending a bridal show, what is most typical for you?

a) I come prepared. I like to print out address labels for information and drawings, and I bring my planner to take notes. I have a list of what I still need, yet I am open to any new ideas I see.

b) I take my time and analyze each vendor. Before arriving, I sometimes look over the vendors attending and visit their websites to see if they fit my budget. At the show, I'm not afraid to talk to vendors and ask them questions about pricing, availability, and their past experience.

c) I spend most of my time admiring the latest linens, dress designs, and floral centerpieces. They are candy for my eyes!

d) I like to enjoy the show with my mom and bridesmaids. I can feel overwhelmed with so many things to look at and vendors to talk to, so it helps me to have others assist in asking questions and helping me select vendors.

As you might be able to tell, the As are answers typical for a Savvy bride, Bs for a Functional bride, Cs for a Visionary bride, and Ds for a Bewildered bride.

Personality Analysis

The second possible way to discern personality is by asking the right questions and analyzing the bride's answers. This can take a little bit of practice, but if it's used every day, it becomes simple to identify personalities!

Following are probing questions that can be extremely effective in identifying a bride's planning personality type. I love using a preprinted sheet with these questions, and I ask them each time a bride calls or meets with me.

Also, it's important to note that these questions and answers are based on trends and not an exact science. The way each bride reacts is purely subjective. However, these typical answers can provide great insight.

Probing Questions:

"What is your vision for your wedding?"
S: She'll most likely know her colors and the feel and vision of her wedding, and will also be specific on what she wants to spend.
F: She'll know the date, time, and guest count as well as the budget, but she probably won't have a clue regarding the look for the day.
V: She'll be able to go into minute detail regarding what she and everyone else is going to look like. Every description will be imbued with emotion and backed up with examples of what she likes. But she may not even think to ask about price or have an established budget.
B: She'll probably either have a long, incohesive list of things she likes and doesn't like, or she won't have any idea at all. She might not have a date selected or a budget set yet. And she just wants everyone to be happy.

"Have you established a budget?"
S: She'll have a certain budget established but may be flexible on it if she finds something that is outstanding.
F: She'll definitely have a set budget and will probably not be flexible. She may even ask what deals you are offering.

V: She may provide you with a number, but more than likely she doesn't have one established. If she sees something that is a "must have," she'll take it!
B: She more than likely doesn't have a budget yet other than what others have told her.

"When are you looking to make a decision?"
S: She has a date in mind of when she'd like to have a decision made and will probably stick to it. She's not going to wait for a very long time, as she knows she needs to book her date quickly.
F: She's not in a rush to find the right vendor that will fit her budget. She may take quite a bit of time researching and isn't afraid to tell you who else she's interviewing.
V: If she likes you, she may hire you on the spot!
B: She can sometimes be so busy or unorganized that she may either book on the spot to cross it off her list or may need some reminding along the way. She may not know when she needs to make a decision.

"What have you liked and not liked at other weddings you have attended?"
S: She'll have plenty of stories to tell you and she'll know exactly what she wants because of it.
F: She may think that a couple overspent, or she might not understand why there was so much floral when it all went to "waste" at the end of the night.
V: She may give many examples of visual items. The centerpieces didn't look fresh, the bridesmaids' dresses didn't match the tuxedo ties, etc.
B: She has probably enjoyed most of the weddings she's attended and just had a good time!

"What are your biggest concerns on the wedding day?"
S: She may have a hard time relaxing and having confidence in all her vendors that everything will be taken care of perfectly to her specifications. She may worry that vendors won't show up on time or deliver what they promise.

F: She can sometimes worry that there will be extra costs on the wedding day. She doesn't like surprises.

V: Her concerns will lie in the beauty of the day. Will her linens match the carpet? Will the white in her bouquet perfectly match the white of her dress?

B: She's concerned about everyone having a good time. Will her mother like the music? Will her friends enjoy the bar? She's worried about the happiness of those around her.

A Savvy can be identified outside of taking the quiz by the way she presents the vision for her wedding. She usually wants to meet right away. She might even say in an e-mail, "Are you available tomorrow?" Or she might just pop in for a visit. She usually knows what she wants when she walks in the door. She has an understanding of what style and budget she wants to maintain. She might also have a wedding date that is further away than other types of brides. If you ask who the decision maker is and she identifies herself, this is another good sign she's a Savvy. Another tip-off would be if she asks you for vendors you recommend. She might ask you how many other events you'll have on her wedding date.

When a Functional bride calls, she most often talks about price, indicating she wants to get a good value. "I don't mind spending money, but I want to be sure I'm getting a good deal for my money." "I know I want a Mercedes, but I can only afford a Volvo. Can you help me achieve that?" "Do you negotiate pricing?" When it comes to the look of the wedding, they typically have no idea. They'll know the date, time, and guest count, but not the wedding colors or vision. "I know I want to add special touches, but I don't know what they are." They also usually indicate they are considering several other vendors in addition to you.

A Visionary bride will describe what she pictures her wedding looking like when you ask her what she wants for her wedding. She typically provides both a visual and an emotional depiction of what she envisions. You'll find that she typically asks for input on what things cost ... or, on the flip side, she may completely ignore that fact altogether. She wants to see as much of your work as possible. "Have you found some really creative places to shoot at this location?" "I want a shot that looks just like this." She'll bring tons of pictures and magazine cut-outs.

Your Bewildered brides might be the most identifiable when gauging by your first impression. They might not have any idea when or where they're getting married, how much they can afford to spend, or what they want the day to look like. She may have someone with her when you first speak with her, or you could speak to one of her "representatives." "I think your place looks really nice, but I have no idea how much anything costs or what I need." "I want everyone to have a great time." "I thought your work looked really great in your ad. I have no idea what you cost or my budget for your service." "I have a bunch of people coming with me, so I have to check their schedules before making an appointment with you." Ultimately, you might walk away from a consultation with a Bewildered not knowing who the decision maker is—or much of anything else.

The questions you ask in your first conversation with a bride are critical for your ability to analyze her personality. Most brides won't answer every single question the same way (for a certain personality), but the previous answers are trends that I've noticed and can provide insight into the personality of a bride.

"Our initial communication to brides has completely changed (due to The Susan Southerland Secret), and we've seen our response rates go from 10 percent to 65 percent in just one week!"—Cameron Fox, chief creative officer, iEntertainment

Chapter 8: Phases of Wedding Planning

Wedding Planning Phases

Marketing and selling to brides isn't necessarily over when your contract is signed. Nor is selling and marketing to brides only done at the beginning of the wedding planning process. There are actually four phases that brides go through when planning their weddings, and by understanding each of these phases and changing your marketing messages accordingly, you'll be able to capture more income. Also keep in mind that selling and marketing will vary by the bride's planning personality (whether she's a Savvy, Functional, Visionary, or Bewildered). Now let's go into more detail about each phase and what we as vendors should be mindful of to maximize success.

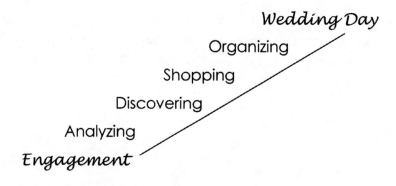

First Phase: Analyzing

The Analyzing Phase is the "preplanning" phase for brides. This is the time when the bride is creating her budget and guest list and deciding what is most important to her. While she is going through this phase, there are certain steps the bride will take. As vendors, there are corresponding things you can do to enhance your marketing at this time.

During this phase, brides are still on the "high" of getting engaged because this is really the beginning of the planning process, and they're going to the typical resources for help in getting started:

1. She'll be at the bookstore buying magazines by the stack.
2. She'll surf the Internet looking for beautiful photos and gathering ideas and inspiration.
3. She'll look for the nearest upcoming bridal shows so that she can use those forums to get to know local vendors.

Sales and marketing has to be done in a variety of ways to achieve the most impact during this phase. To maximize your reach, make sure you have:

1. Attractive, well-placed ads in local wedding magazines
2. A beautiful, visible website that ranks high on Google searches
3. Participation in bridal shows; figure out the best components to include in a bridal show booth or display to make you stand out from your competition.

Let's discuss each of these ideas in a bit more detail. During the Analyzing Phase, keep these concepts in mind:

- *Know some basic points about advertising.*
    o Your ads should have a phone number, a web address, and social networking information. You want to make yourself as accessible to potential clients as possible.

o   Use logos and colors consistently so that your brand is always recognizable. I recommend using no more than three fonts in your logo, website, and advertisement.

o   Have engaging photos in your ads to convey your brand and create interest in your product or service. Keep in mind that just because we as vendors think a certain picture markets us best, it doesn't necessarily equate to what a bride is seeking. People tend to lean toward pictures that showcase emotion rather than tangible items. Tangible items will only appeal toward some brides (such as Savvies or Visionaries). Intangible items such as emotion never go out of style and are attractive to any type of bride.

o   Review all current advertising and ensure photos and contact information are up-to-date.

o   Don't expect your ad to do all the work. Take part in a leads programs and do mail or e-mail blasts to get your marketing message out to potential clients. It's important to have a solid lead list organization process. Some vendors find it easy to use online programs while others use simple spreadsheets. Whichever you choose, ensure you are using them effectively.

Where can you receive lead lists?

And what will you do with these lead lists?

- *Follow these tips for an effective website:*
  o Flash templates are a very popular and cost-effective way to create a website, but keep in mind that some people can't view these types of sites on their smartphones. This could decrease your site's effectiveness.
  o Make sure photos are of the highest quality and evoke emotion and interest in the viewer. Sometimes it can be better to have fewer pictures that are of better quality than having a plethora of poor quality pictures.
  o Put the most important information and most impressive photos toward the top of the site so that the viewer doesn't have to scroll down to see them.
  o Make sure the website is easily navigated/user-friendly.
  o Have others review your site and get opinions on how easily they were able to get information (were the photos interesting, was the content cohesive, etc.).
  o Include testimonials as frequently as possible.
  o Ensure your contact information is on every single page.

- *Some thoughts on bridal shows*:
  o Check out the source of the show. Make sure it's being run by a reputable company.
  o Find out how the show is being promoted.
  o Get references and discuss the success of prior shows with other vendors within your market.
  o Find out if and when you will receive the list of brides and their contact information so you can promote to them before and after the show.
  o Promote that you're going to be at the show to all of your inquiries, as well as on your social networking pages and your website. If possible, send out an e-mail blast to your lead list to let them know you'll be there, and encourage them to attend.

o	Set goals for the outcome of the bridal show. Don't necessarily expect to sign contracts at the show, but be prepared to set appointments and follow-up meetings.
o	Create a "call to action" while at the show. What do you want a bride to do (other than book!) that's reasonable to expect from a bridal show?

Second Phase: Discovering
The Discovering Phase is when the bride is coming up with her overall look and vision for the wedding. She's making choices on color, the style and location of the wedding, and what type of party she's planning to have, and coming up with the ideas of the elements for the look and feel of the wedding. At this point, brides are tearing out and printing their favorite photos, they're reading articles and blogs, and they're actually now attending bridal shows and other wedding-related events.

During this phase, vendors should make sure to have great photos on the Internet and in magazines. Take advantage of easily updated services such as Flickr, Facebook, and YouTube. Start writing a blog and try to write publishable articles for magazines in addition to beefing up your social networking presence. Brides are always looking for new and fresh content, as are magazines and newspapers. Finally, get more visible by attending local bridal shows.

-	*Make good use of photos and video*
	o	Flickr, in particular, is recognized by search engines, so if you don't have an account, get one.
	o	Upload good photographs. If you aren't talented behind the camera, partner with some local photographers in your area and ask to exchange some of their work for photo credit wherever you use the photos.
	o	Use photos whenever you make Facebook or Twitter posts; this makes each post more interesting and relevant.

- o Use YouTube to make attention-grabbing instructional or behind-the-scenes videos.
- o Make sure to tag and title photos and videos in an effective manner. This will drive the right viewers who are searching for your keywords to your site to view your work.

- *Get your message out there through articles, blogs, and social networking*
    - o If writing isn't a strength of yours, partner with someone who is a good writer. You can come up with ideas and the writer can help you craft them into something marketable.
    - o Always check for grammar and spelling. Never put something out there isn't 100 percent polished.
    - o Get to know publishers and editors in your area to discuss submitting material.
    - o When you create your own blog, make sure you have a goal for it. Are you just giving advice? Are you showing examples of your work? Or are you using it as a sales and marketing tool? Then stick to that goal.
    - o Title and tag your blog posts to drive traffic back to your website.
    - o Always post engaging photos with your blogs.
    - o Invite the reader to make comments and respond to those comments. The more conversation on each blog post, the higher and more frequently you'll rank in the search engines.
    - o Use Facebook and Twitter to start conversations, not just as billboards to announce what you're doing for the day. Keep in mind that many brides block vendors that constantly post all day long about every little thing. Make sure your posts are interesting; a sprinkling of personal posts can be very endearing.

- *Working the bridal shows*
  - o Create an interesting and inviting booth. Ask yourself if it's visually appealing, if it will stand out from other booths, and if you have an attractive, visible offer.
  - o Use your logos and colors for easy brand recognition.
  - o Consider offering incentives to brides who book your services at the show.
  - o Get excited while at the show so that you present yourself as someone with whom the bride wants to do business.
  - o Capture names and contact information. Even though you may get a lead list after the show, create a way that you can capture specifically interested prospects.
  - o Use your time wisely! Vendors generally have only a minute or two to catch the potential bride's interest. Be organized and prepared to use that time effectively.
  - o Follow up with all contacts after the show.

Third Phase: Shopping

The Shopping Phase is when brides are making their final selections. They're actually going out to businesses and sitting and speaking with vendors in preparation for signing contracts. At this point, the bride is having in-person meetings, she's choosing her vendors, and she's negotiating contracts.

As a wedding vendor, you need to have a professional, welcoming location to meet with brides while reinforcing your business messages. If you have an office, you should have your work surrounding you. But even if you don't have a regular meeting place and you're meeting at the local coffee shop, for example, make sure that you have promotional items available. Take good notes during the meeting, and when negotiating the contract, be aware of what the bride says that she wants but might not be able to afford just then.

During this phase, you should also have your business information available in other vendors' locations and have other vendors' information available at your venue. One of the most successful cross-marketing endeavors I've ever seen was among a florist, a linen company, and a lighting company. Each of them had large areas for displays at their individual locations, so in every office, they had a table completely set with beautiful linens, a gorgeous silk centerpiece arrangement, and the perfect lighting. Every time I'd take a client through one of these vendors' offices, the client would immediately say, "Wow. Who did those linens (or lighting, or centerpiece)?" Nearly every time that I booked one of those vendors' services, the client usually wound up booking with the other vendors as well, even if it went outside of their initial budget. When it comes to weddings, nothing sells better than having an actual display of what the bride can get. So, if you have items to sell, make sure they're prominently displayed!

Lastly, during this phase you should be sure to get the bride's e-mail, phone number, and snail mail information at the face-to-face meeting. It's very rare to make a sale right on the spot. So follow-up is key. The follow-up process may take longer or be more involved than a simple e-mail after the sales meeting, so make sure to get as much contact information as possible.

- *Create an inviting space that truly represents your service*
  o Make an excellent first impression by making sure your meeting space is neat and orderly. And don't meet anywhere that doesn't have clean bathrooms!
  o Try to avoid meeting in noisy or distracting locations. If the local coffee shop is too busy, try a picnic table in a nearby park with fresh lemonade and cookies in the summer, or a luxury department store café with a glass of champagne.
  o Offer the bride samples and photos of your work.
  o Extend hospitality by offering potential clients a beverage or something to eat.
  o Be sure that everything the bride looks at has your logos and colors to reinforce your brand.
  o Offer her testimonials from former clients.

o If you're meeting in a public space, make sure you have a solid presentation so that the bride really gets to know you and your work in that short span of time.

- *Cross-market with fellow vendors*
    o Exchange business cards or flyers with other vendors and make theirs available for brides who come to meet you.
    o Keep in mind that this is an opportunity to get seen for free. Can you provide other vendors with anything that will help them sell themselves? A nice arrangement, a picture for their wall? A special "sales" mixed CD to play during consultations?
    o Maintain good company. Be sure you know the companies and vendors with which you choose to cross-market. You and your business will be closely associated with theirs, so you want to be sure you have similar business philosophies.
    o Having the information of other vendors available for brides to review makes you a credible resource for brides to turn to when needed. It also extends to other vendors a gesture of goodwill, increasing networking efficiency.

- *Get contact information*
    o Brides today require more information before making their decisions, so follow-up may be the deciding factor between losing business and getting the signed contract. It may seem like a lot to ask for addresses and everyone's correct spelling of their names, but it will come in handy when wanting to send a handwritten thank-you note or postcard.
    o Functional and Savvy brides, in particular, really like to weigh their decisions. So showing them continued interest in their business through useful follow-up may be just the thing that sways them in the direction to sign your contract.

- o Useful follow-up is *not* repeated e-mails asking if they've made a decision and if they'll sign the contract.
- o Useful follow-up *is* sending brides helpful planning tidbits, such as an article pertaining to one of her concerns or interests mentioned in the initial meeting with her. This is a productive and unobtrusive way to maintain your selling presence with the bride. You can also send electronic newsletters once a month that brides can sign up for, or mail postcards with special offers. Ensure that each form of communication has a goal and a call to action for each bride.

Phase Four: Organizing

By the time you get to the Organizing Phase, the bride has signed the majority of her contracts. She has established the bulk of her wedding day agenda, she's planning how her rehearsal is going to go, she's figuring out when all of her payments are due and how much she's spent, and her mind has gone to organizing the day itself by creating seating charts and adding finishing touches to her plans. At this point, she's getting anxious about how the wedding day will go and she's making sure that she has everything she needs.

You may think that the time for selling is over at this phase. However, that is definitely not the case. Many brides realize at the last minute that they actually have extra money to spend and that they'd like a little something more. So maybe a service or element that they passed up during the initial phases of planning becomes of interest to them now.

As an example, a marketing-savvy videographer with whom I often work recognized that he was having a slow month as the year drew to a close. He proposed offering his services to my brides getting married that month for free to capture the ceremony footage. He then edited the footage down to a short clip to send the couple, including my contact information and his own at the conclusion of the clip. He also indicated that the full video was available for purchase if the couple was interested. This creative effort resulted in immediate sales that he otherwise wouldn't have had.

Vendors should be mindful during the Organizing Phase that outreach through mail and e-mail could result in last-minute sales. If you took good notes during the Shopping Phase, you can reach out to her now to remind her of some of the items she wanted to have but couldn't at that time. You have to decide if you want to try and maximize sales by offering special last-minute discounts. Depending on the type of vendor you are, there is still an opportunity to make your services more enticing to brides who may have initially turned you down.

- *Final outreach*
   o Brides are commonly seeking to enhance their weddings with final touches during this phase. Thus, mail and e-mails targeting brides who had at one time expressed an interest could definitely capture their business now.

> What can you sell to brides
> 3 months out?
> Thirty days out? Two weeks out?
>
> Which personalities will that interest most?
>
> How will you communicate
> these sellable options to these personalities?

   o In your communication with brides, try to focus on their interests and their wedding vision to make your services as appealing as possible to them.

o   Make your final pitch personal and personable. Tell her you hope her planning is going well, and you would love to help make her day even better.

o   Possibly offer her some last-minute advice that will endear her to you.

o   Ask for the sale. Ask if you can hold her date for a week while she makes her final decision, or ask to send a contract. For some brides, this is all it takes to make their decision.

- *Upsell*

o   By this phase, you as a vendor should have a good understanding of what each bride has contracted and what might have interested her but she didn't book.

o   Send her a photo or video clip of services that you know captured her attention during the initial planning phases to try and rekindle that interest.

- *Discounting*

o   Whether or not you offer special pricing for last-minute bookings is up to you. Decide whether this fits in with your overall business plan and philosophy.

o   Last-minute discounts and special offers can be very effective tools for closing the sale, especially during this final phase.

Table 2: Effective Marketing Methods by Planning Personality

Savvy	Functional	Visionary	Bewildered
Have clean and professional ads and collateral showcasing emotion Consistently post blogs, Facebook, and Twitter updates and encourage interaction via social media Have previous work to show her at your bridal show booth and have a strategy of how to get her to talk with you; what are you providing her at the show?	Use words such as "discount" or "special offer" or "save" in marketing materials Utilize testimonials from brides and other vendors that highly rate your work Offer incentives at the bridal show	Showcase professionally shot design pictures Provide her tangible things that enhance her senses at your bridal show booth Post pictures online on your blog, Facebook, and Flickr accounts; if possible, upload some videos to YouTube for DIY projects Put slideshows together with powerful music	Follow up in a variety of ways—e-mails, phone calls, and postcards can remind her, but be careful not to overwhelm her When sending out information for a consultation "call to action," invite family and friends to attend with her Encourage her to sign up for your e-mail newsletter that has ideas on how to save and how to make a wedding beautiful

We've now discussed all four phases of wedding planning. The most important thing vendors need to know to effectively reach today's brides is how to identify each bride's personality, needs, and worries. Reach out to her in a number of ways at varying times using a variety of methods. And remember that you're never done selling. Even when the client has signed your contract, you need to provide her service in a way that will make her enthusiastically refer you to other people, as well as be open to purchasing more from you. If the client trusts you and likes you, that one sale can blossom into an abundance of future sales.

Chapter 9: Susan's Short and Sweets

*A*s a result of presenting The Susan Southerland Secret to various wedding vendors across the country, I have developed a few tips specific to most of the major vendor categories. These quick tips are designed to maximize a vendor's marketing and sales strategies. Always remember: change doesn't have to be significant to realize a significant result!

Videographers: Cultivate relationships with other successful vendors. During slow times, offer your services pro bono to another vendor's brides, sending a "teaser clip" of the footage to the bride with your brand as well as the other vendor's brand included. Encourage the bride (or guests seeking a unique wedding gift for the couple) to contact you after the wedding to purchase the full video. This will secure bookings you otherwise wouldn't have had and will allow you to build a strong portfolio. You can also consider selling the raw footage for a special rate.

Photographers: Have do-it-yourself options available. Scrapbooking is incredibly popular right now. You can offer partially completed albums at a reduced price, saving you time and generating more income.

DJs: With today's brides often deciding to use iPods, offer sound systems and other equipment for rent to couples. Also, share how their guests can be part of the experience. This is particularly fun for couples getting married who have children. Children love being part of the party!

Wardrobe: Offer professional stylists to guide brides in their purchases. Also, don't neglect to offer additional services such as gown

preservation, shoes, and accessories so brides can make most of their big purchases in one place. She can always return to the salon at a later date.

Florists: Consider offering fresh-cut flowers and embellishments (ribbon, crystals, feathers, brooches, monograms, etc.) for do-it-yourself brides. Have these readily available for brides to see in your studio. Viewing pictures is nice, but being able to see and feel things in person can engage a bride on the spot!

Stationers: Offer embellishments that will allow brides to make their stationery more personalized. Carry lines of stationery in all price ranges. Also, consider offering DIY options. Most brides have printers and may prefer to print things themselves. Instead of losing the sale altogether, have some options available in the back of your studio in case you can still get the sale by selling the paper products.

Wedding Planners: Shorten your labor time and offer reduced rates. Offer phone and online consultations for brides who are looking for guidance during the planning process, but may not want to commit to full-service planning. Once the bride sees how helpful you are, she may upgrade to include more of your services. Also, teach a group wedding-planning

seminar at your favorite reception location. If you keep individual fees reasonable and do a great job marketing the event, you may make the same amount of money in just one evening that you would have planning one wedding.

Venues: Keep reusable wedding items such as arches and arbors in stock, or possibly offer décor options that incur a per-person charge, such as chair linens or reusable centerpieces. A great item to have available for upgrades is

Chiavari chairs. Team up with a linen-rental company and offer a variety of linens to rent to your clients.

Officiants: Provide unity ceremony items for sale and offer assistance with acquiring the marriage license. Also, offer resources such as books that inspire vows and other elements for the wedding ceremony. If you have a talent for writing, offer a custom vow-writing service to your couples.

Styling Services: False eyelashes are huge right now. Suggest these as you are getting the bride ready for the big day. Offer "mini-touch-up" kits for purchase or, better yet, offer to extend your time so that you can touch up everyone's makeup between the ceremony and reception. Other possible add-ons could include hair embellishments, facials, or skin-care products. Teaming up with an aesthetician can also beef up your sales.

All Vendors: Offer flexible payment options, especially if the planning time frame is long.

If you don't currently accept credit cards, consider doing it. Some consumers will make purchases more quickly if they have the option to put it on their credit cards. If you don't want to invest in merchant services, use PayPal, (www.PayPal.com) or Square (www.SquareUp.com). Square provides a device that you can attach to your mobile phone or tablet. Wherever you have access to the Internet, you have the ability to run credit cards.

Chapter 10: Bringing It All Together

I look back on the days when I went blindly into potential client meetings without a strategy, simply hoping the bride liked me. Every time I received a signed contract, I couldn't help but wonder if it would be the last wedding I ever booked. After identifying and analyzing the different planning personalities, however, I now have much more confidence in not only talking with brides, but in strategically selling to them. My company's increased revenue and the reduction of overall stress levels prove that planning ahead is highly effective ... and it will work for you!

While society may look at weddings as an industry filled with fairytales and romance, we as vendors know that it's actually a lot of hard work. We all spend sleepless nights fearing what our bank accounts currently look like, worrying about how many weddings we'll book for the upcoming year, and wondering how to deal with "challenging" brides. Furthermore, we're mostly small business owners looking to increase our income in a market that sprouts up new competitors every day.

You're probably now asking yourself how you can combat this. Quite simply, you have to take the first step in changing the way you do business. It's time to change how you perceive brides and consider how your income will increase through this renewed perspective. And now you have the perfect resource to help you along the way.

The Susan Southerland Secret was designed to offer insight on marketing organically for appropriate leads, customizing sales to encourage those leads to sign the contract, and effectively planning with a variety of brides and grooms in a high-tech world. Now it's time for you to take these ideas and implement them in your own business. I know you'll be excited when you see results right away!

"I love your … approach on how to deal with our clients, especially our brides. Right after your presentation, I was able to apply some of those great ideas with a prospective bride and was able to book my next wedding immediately with very little effort. Thank you so much for sharing your knowledge with the rest of us. Our industry needs more people like you."—Lucmann Pierre, owner/ executive chef, Le Pierre Caterers, LLC

Appendix A (Planning Personality Quiz)

1. **If you were a volunteer on a committee to plan a party, what job would you want to have?**

   - O A - I would be president! I like to oversee all aspects of the party and have a good grasp on budgeting, decorating, and delegating.
   - O B - I would lead the creative efforts. My passion lies in selecting a theme and designing the overall look. My ideas are endless!
   - O C - I would be responsible for operations. I enjoy researching all the little details such as the location, date, and vendors. And I'm good when it comes to ensuring we stay on track with our budget!
   - O D - I prefer to help out wherever the team needs me. In planning a party, it's better if I receive direction from those planning it!

2. **How would best describe your planning experience so far?**

   - O A - A breeze! I could do this all of the time.
   - O B - A dream when it comes to designing the look of the day. It's just so difficult to remember to stay within our budget!
   - O C - Fun when researching venues and vendors. I just wish I knew what to tell them when they ask what our special day will look like.
   - O D - I think I need some help. My life is so busy that I don't know what to do next and I'm becoming overwhelmed!

3. **When planning a date night with your fiancé, what are you most likely to do?**

   O A - Plan ahead! I am most likely to make reservations a few weeks prior, lay out his clothes, and surprise him with his favorite drink when he walks in the door after work.

   O B - Have a blast! I'm up for anything as long as I have enough time to pick out the perfect outfit and accessories. Sometimes a quick trip to the mall beforehand for cute shoes is just a must!

   O C - Prioritize! I tend to look at my "going out budget" and then select a restaurant that fits it nicely. I also like to read the latest reviews on new movies or attractions before deciding.

   O D - Ask my fiancé what he would like to do and decide together. I can sometimes have a hard time making decisions on restaurants or entertainment, so his input is greatly appreciated!

4. **When picturing your wedding day, what are you most likely to worry about?**

   O A - Being able to hand off all the details that I so carefully planned for the day. I'm just worried the person overseeing my day won't be able to coordinate it to my expectations.

   O B - That my set-up may not look nice. I'm not an expert at color swatches and floral selection, never mind lighting and linens. I hope that the look comes together okay.

   O C - My budget. I'm concerned that I have overspent and am afraid to get the bills after the big day.

   O D - Everything and everyone. I hope that everyone likes it even though I had a difficult time selecting the décor. And I don't think I want to know what I spent, but as long as everyone is happy, that's all that matters.

5. **How would you best describe yourself during the wedding planning process?**

   O A - Everything is organized perfectly and I am *the* expert at putting my designs together. I love to find inspiration and then make it work to fit my budget.

   O B - I may not keep a formal budget or exactly know where to find my vendor contracts, but I can tell you the exact color of my bridesmaid dresses, the designer, and what flowers I'm considering for their complementing bouquets.

   O C - I am pretty well organized and can negotiate to ensure I find the best deals. However, I have a hard time choosing colors and patterns. I tend to need help with the creative side of my wedding.

   O D - I wish I could be organized, but don't quite know where to start. And I could use some help with designing, but who do I ask exactly?

6. **When you go shopping with friends, what are you most likely to do?**

   O A - Even though my friends may like to shop in many stores, I know exactly the ones that I prefer and have the latest coupon that was mailed to me.

   O B - Spend just as much time looking for accessories as I do for my major basics. I am even known to bring a dress or pair of shoes with me in order to find the perfect matching item!

   O C - I like to start by window shopping. I have a good idea of what I can spend and I want to see what deals are out there first before I commit to anything.

   O D - Ask my friends for advice! I love to get their opinions on what looks good on me or what to pair with a skirt I've owned for a year and have yet to wear.

7. **When attending a bridal show, what is most typical of you?**

   O A - I take my time. Before arriving, I sometimes look over the vendors attending and visit some of their websites to see if they fit my budget. At the show, I am not afraid to talk to vendors and ask them questions about pricing, date availability, and their past experience.

   O B - I spend most of my time admiring the latest linens, dress designs, and floral centerpieces. It's like candy for my eyes!

   O C - I come prepared. I like to print out address labels for information and drawings, and I bring my planner to take notes. I have a list of what I still need, yet I am open to any new ideas I see as well!

   O D - I like to enjoy the show with my mom and bridesmaids. I can feel overwhelmed with so many things to look at and vendors to talk to so it helps me to have others assist in asking questions and picking out new styles.

8. **If you were asked to bring a beverage to a dinner party you were attending, what are you most likely to do?**

   O A - Find the perfect pairing that everyone will be talking about! I would first ask the host what is being served and then select the perfect complementing beverage—looking for quality at a somewhat reasonable price, of course.

   O B - Get the party started! I love to stroll aisle by aisle looking for the most beautiful label or cutest name. It gets people taking and puts a smile on their faces as soon as I arrive. That is priceless, so I don't usually worry about the cost.

   O C - Review and budget! I am known to research online or read the review tabs hanging on store shelves for a selection in only my specified budget.

   O D - Ask for assistance! With my busy schedule, I find it helpful to ask a store manager for his recommendations as I stop in on my way to the party. He knows what is good in his selection, right? I just hold my breath when he rings it up!

9. **At your menu tasting, what is most likely to be your main focus?**

    O A - Details, details, details! My favorite parts include the presentation of food, selecting my napkin fold, and reviewing the overall table setup. I like to see what the linen, silverware, glasses, and plates look like together and whether I'll need chair covers.

    O B - Well, I have been dreaming about this since the day I got engaged! I make sure I have my planner to take notes in and bring a camera to take pictures to remember the experience. I'm not intimidated to ask the chef if I can switch out the filet for something less expensive or ask for his/her suggestions on unique beverage pairings.

    O C - As most of my budget is going toward food and beverage for my guests, I want to make sure it is money well spent. I have a tendency to ask why there is a "cake-cutting fee" and if a "hosted bar" is more economical than an "open bar." At the end, I request a proposal from the catering manager outlining all my estimated costs.

    O D - Everything! I have never been to a menu tasting before and have no idea what to expect, so I look to the guidance of the catering manager to walk me through it all.

10. **What planning "tool" do you find most helpful as you get ready for the big day?**

    O A - My wedding planning binder. It has *everything* I need! Whether it's a place to hold my magazine cutouts, my vendors' business cards, or my guest list organizer, I can take it all with me anywhere I go.

    O B - Wedding magazines. I look forward to receiving them each month and on the day they arrive, I plan a relaxing soak in the tub and spend the night *ooh*ing and *ahh*ing over each page! I love the ideas and sometimes it makes me want to change what I have already picked.

    O C - My computer. I have organized my guest list, timeline, and budget in up-to-date spreadsheets. I have electronic files where I can find things such as scanned contracts, online receipts, and favorite links to wedding vendors.

O D - My family and friends. I love to get advice from everyone—especially those who have planned a wedding before. It helps ease my worry about picking the right things!

11. **You have just moved into a new home. What are you most likely to do first?**

O A - Create a theme! I find it most helpful to decide on an overall theme for each area of the house and then plan accordingly. It gives me guidance on the style I am looking for as I search stores for specially priced items.

O B - Paint and decorate! Before even signing the papers, I have picked out paint colors and have already begun to purchase wall hangings and furniture. I can't stop looking through decor books. I want it all!

O C - Wait and review. Instead of shopping right away, I like to live in my new home for a few weeks to get acquainted with it. I make a list of things I'm missing and then, after I've saved up, I shop for items that provide great function in my everyday life.

O D - Host an unpacking party. This way, I can get input of my friends and family regarding what looks best where—and I don't have to sit there staring at all of those boxes that would go unpacked if it were up to me!

12. **What do you find the most challenging part of your wedding planning thus far?**

O A - Taking everyone's advice! I have a great vision of what I want and it's important to me that our special day represents both me and my fiancé. I have been dreaming about this for as long as I can remember and I'm good at making my own decisions.

O B - Definitely staying within a budget! I can't help but love all of the creative aspects of the wedding, but I just dread looking at the bills and figuring out who is going to sit where.

○ C - Describing the look of the day. I am at a loss when deciding on all the artistic elements such as what dress color best represents my skin tone (what's the difference between ivory and ivory white?) and deciding on miniature roses vs. spray roses for the corsages (aren't they the same thing?).

○ D - Pretty much everything! I'm too busy to spend a lot of time planning my wedding and when I do, I don't know where to start!

Scoring:

Mostly As - You are a Savvy bride! You have a keen sense of what your day will look like and how to manage it. You are organized from the start! You stick to a timeline and book vendors, location, invitations, etc., as soon as possible. Knowing almost exactly what you want, your expectations are high and you may be on the lookout for the latest trends to exceed those expectations.

Mostly Bs - You are a Visionary bride! You can picture your perfect day. You are pretty sure of what your colors will be, the names of your flowers, and the location is a given. But when it is time to look at the logistics of the day, it makes you cringe! You may not have created a budget or don't necessarily know where to start with one. It can sometimes be challenging to stay on task or meet deadlines with contracts (if you can find them!). And you may question whether or not you really need a formal agenda for the day, as you are sure it will all come together ... somehow.

Mostly Cs - You are a Functional bride! You are very good at the logistics of planning your day. You could be described as detail oriented or a task master, you are analytical, and you may like to stick to a timeline. However, when it comes to making your wedding day visually stunning, you may not have a sure sense of where to start. It may be challenging to make decisions about colors, flowers, and linens, and you may have a hard time defining your true style.

Mostly Ds - You are a Bewildered bride! As excited as you are about being engaged, you may not know where to begin. You may be too busy with your daily life to spend much time planning, or when you do have time, you don't know what to do first. You are looking for simple ideas that won't take too much time to accomplish but will keep you on task *or* you need assistance with both making your wedding beautiful and keeping it organized!

References

"The American Wedding [Survey]," Fairchild Bridal Group, last modified August 16, 2004, accessed January 22, 2011, http://www.sellthebride.com/documents/americanweddingsurvey.pdf.

"Global Advertising: Consumers Trust Real Friends and Virtual Strangers the Most," last modified July 7, 2009, accessed January 22, 2011, http://blog.nielsen.com/nielsenwire/...

R. A. Zaldivar, "Move Over, Generation X; 'Echo Boomers' Poised to Rule the World," last modified March 8, 1998, accessed July 14, 2010, http://www.thefreelibrary.com/MOVE+OVER,+GENERATION+X%3 B+%60 ECHO+BOOMERS%27+POISED+TO+RULE+THE+ WORLD. -a083814544).

Author Biographies

Susan Southerland
Celebrity wedding planner and vendor consultant Susan Southerland is one of the foremost experts in the wedding industry today. She boasts the honor of planning thousands of weddings, and now she helps other vendors achieve the same success. Susan is president of Just Marry!, a full service wedding planning company with offices in Orlando, Florida. Her exceptional weddings have been featured numerous times on the Style Network's "Whose Wedding Is It Anyway?" and TLC's "A Wedding Story." Her cutting-edge advice has been seen on television stations around the country as well as *The Wall Street Journal, The New York Times, The Orlando Sentinel, Orlando Leisure*, and *The Orlando Business Journal*.

Most recently, she was asked to become the National Wedding Expert for the nationally renowned wedding publication and online resource, *Perfect Wedding Guide*. With *PWG*, she travels the country speaking to brides and vendors on her revolutionary wedding-planning personality concept, The Susan Southerland Secret. Her webinars are viewed daily by brides across the country and vendors looking to revitalize their paradigms for marketing and selling to today's bride.

Her expertise is so widely recognized and loved, she was even given the prestigious recognition as one of only thirty wedding planners worldwide as an "A-List Planner" by *Destination Weddings & Honeymoons Magazine*.

Susan currently consults to both brides and vendors to provide stress-free planning processes. Her advice can be heard at conferences such as Wedding MBA and CaterSource, as well as local seminars throughout the country for those who want to make weddings once-in-a-lifetime experiences.

Kristy Chenell

Known for her inspiring ideas and innovative concepts, Kristy Chenell consults nationwide as one of the wedding industry's leading experts in branding, marketing, and sales strategies. She is the owner of the nationally recognized branding and wedding planning company, Couture Consulting. Kristy began her career at Disney's Fairy Tale Weddings, where she consulted with hundreds of wedding couples, planning weddings at five distinct wedding venues, four theme parks, and seventeen resorts. This unique experience included in-depth brand marketing, website redesign, creation of wedding planning guides, and the television premier of ABC's *Extreme Makeover: Wedding Edition.*

Kristy went on to heighten her wedding experience with The Ritz-Carlton Hotel Company, where she planned Ritz-Carlton Intimate and Signature Weddings with The Ritz-Carlton Orlando, Grande Lakes, as senior wedding sales manager. She then opened The Ritz-Carlton, Denver, as the director of catering sales. Leading her teams in consulting, she wrote and produced a wedding-planning book that was benchmarked by the company for its website. Shortly thereafter, Kristy became one of six people in the country to sit on The Ritz-Carlton Corporate Wedding Advisory Board, where she specialized in designing signature wedding planning experiences with preferred vendors.

Kristy's experience also ranges from work with *Modern Bride Magazine* to Florida's bid for the 2012 Olympic Games. She has been the holiday and wedding expert for Denver's news channel 7, news channel 2, and news channel 4, sharing meaningful holiday décor and wedding design concepts for every type of budget. Kristy travels nationwide to provide one-of-a-kind branding, marketing, and sales solutions to wedding vendors looking to increase sales, work more efficiently, and strive to achieve their dreams. More information about Kristy's services can be found at www.couture-consulting.com.

Karen Gingerich, MA, PHR

As a writer, editor, wedding planner, and business manager, Karen Gingerich has helped build small companies into hugely successful businesses for over fifteen years. A certified professional in human resources with an extensive background in management and administration, she understands how to implement effective business strategies and create winning teams. She has learned that certain business tactics hold true regardless of the industry, and it always takes the human element and fresh perspectives to make success happen.

Karen's passion for all things literary led her to earn her bachelor's degree in English with a focus on Creative Writing from Georgia State University and her master of arts degree in Humanities from Central Michigan University. A member of the Society for Human Resource Management, the Editorial Freelancer's Association, the National Notary Association, and Romance Writers of America, Karen has edited and cowritten numerous articles, booklets, and novels in a variety of genres and disciplines. She has written grants that generated millions of dollars in revenue for nonprofit organizations serving in-need children and adolescents, and recently completed work on a young adult fiction trilogy.

Currently, Karen supervises an amazing team of wedding planners serving brides in central Florida and around the globe. Combined with her experience as a wedding officiant, her planning background has lent her a honed understanding of the ways today's brides and grooms think. She has helped plan hundreds of weddings in her years with Just Marry! and has developed useful strategies to make every bride's experience unique and memorable, whatever her budget.

CPSIA information can be obtained at www.ICGtesting.com
Printed in the USA
LVOW040753130911

245994LV00003B/2/P